GEORGE WASHINGTON

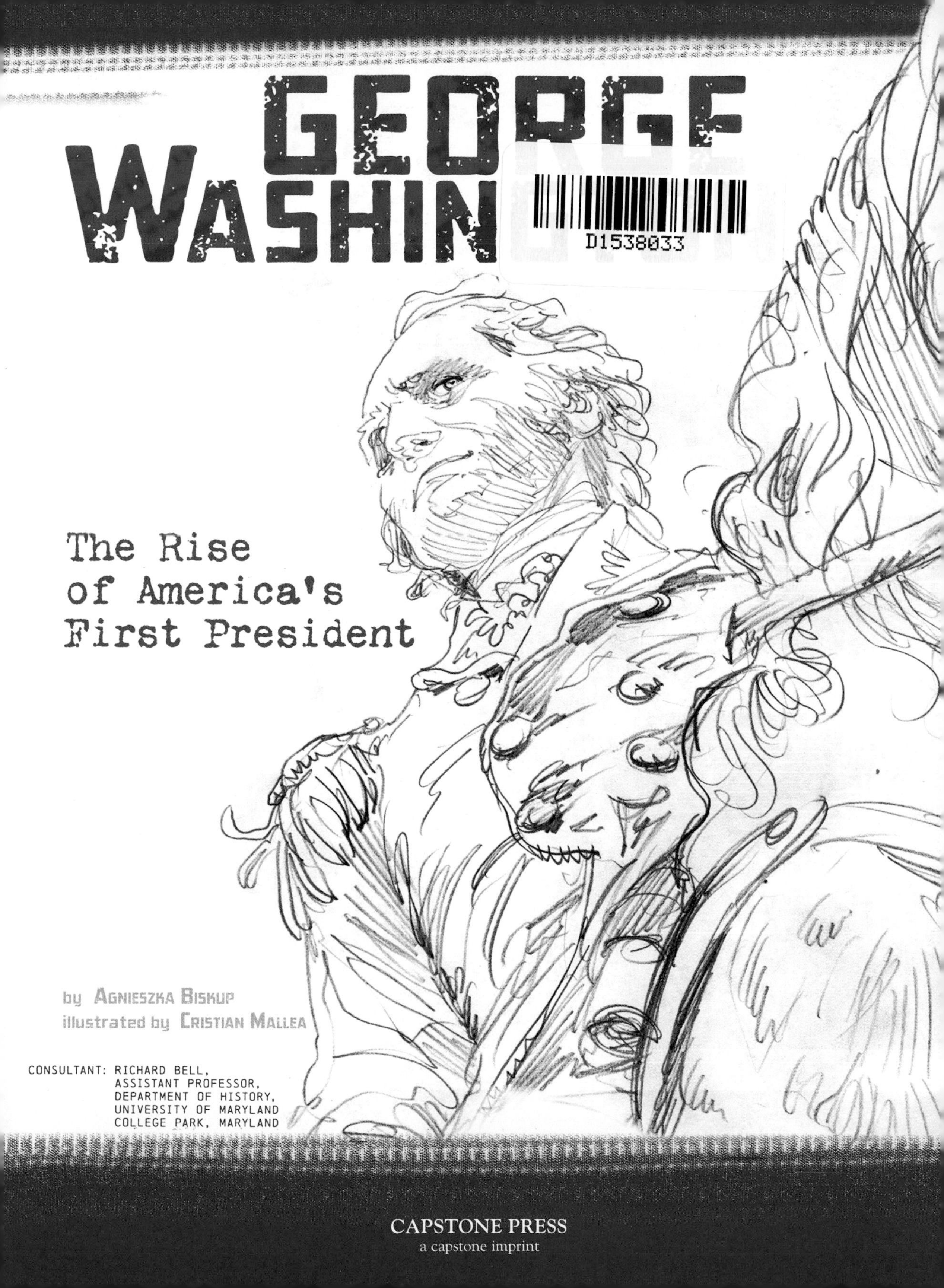

The Rise of America's First President

by Agnieszka Biskup
illustrated by Cristian Mallea

CONSULTANT: RICHARD BELL,
ASSISTANT PROFESSOR,
DEPARTMENT OF HISTORY,
UNIVERSITY OF MARYLAND
COLLEGE PARK, MARYLAND

CAPSTONE PRESS
a capstone imprint

Graphic Library is published by Capstone Press,
1710 Roe Crest Drive
North Mankato, Minnesota 56003
www.capstonepub.com

Library of Congress Cataloging-in-Publication Data
Biskup, Agnieszka.
 George Washington : the rise of America's first
president / by Agnieszka Biskup.
   p. cm. — (Graphic library. American graphics)
 Includes bibliographical references and index.
 Summary: "Describes the life of George Washington,
focusing on his service during the Revolutionary War and
his presidential inauguration"—Provided by publisher.
  ISBN 978-1-4296-8621-1 (library binding)
  ISBN 978-1-4296-9334-9 (paperback)
  ISBN 978-1-62065-266-4 (ebook PDF)
 1. Washington, George, 1732–1799—Comic books,
strips, etc.—Juvenile literature. 2. Presidents—United
States—Biography—Comic books, strips, etc.—Juvenile
literature. 3. Graphic novels. I. Title.

 E312.66.B57 2013
 973.4'1092—dc23
 [B]   2011046830

Image Credit: Library of Congress: Prints and
Photographs Division, 29

Direct quotes appear on the following pages in red:

4, 9, 13 (top), 26 from *Washington: A Life*, by Ron
Chernow (New York: Penguin Press, 2010).

11 from *The Writings of George Washington: Being
His Correspondence, Addresses, Messages, and Other
Papers, Official and Private, Selected and Published from
the Original Manuscripts with a Life of the Author, Notes
and Illustrations*, by Jared Sparks (Boston: American
Stationers' Company, John B. Russell, 1834–1837).

13 (bottom), 19 from *The Papers of George Washington.
Revolutionary War Series*, edited by Philander D. Chase
(Charlottesville: University Press of Virginia, 1985).

16 (both) from "Battles of Trenton and Princeton,"
Rediscovering George Washington, January 10, 2012
(www.pbs.org/georgewashington/).

25 from "Readings by Larry Arnn: Letter to
Lewis Nicola," Rediscovering George Washington,
January 10, 2012 (www.pbs.org/georgewashington/).

Art Director: Nathan Gassman

Editor: Mari Bolte

Production Specialist: Laura Manthe

Printed in the United States of America in Stevens Point, Wisconsin.
032016   009602R

TABLE OF CONTENTS

CHAPTER 1 The President-Elect

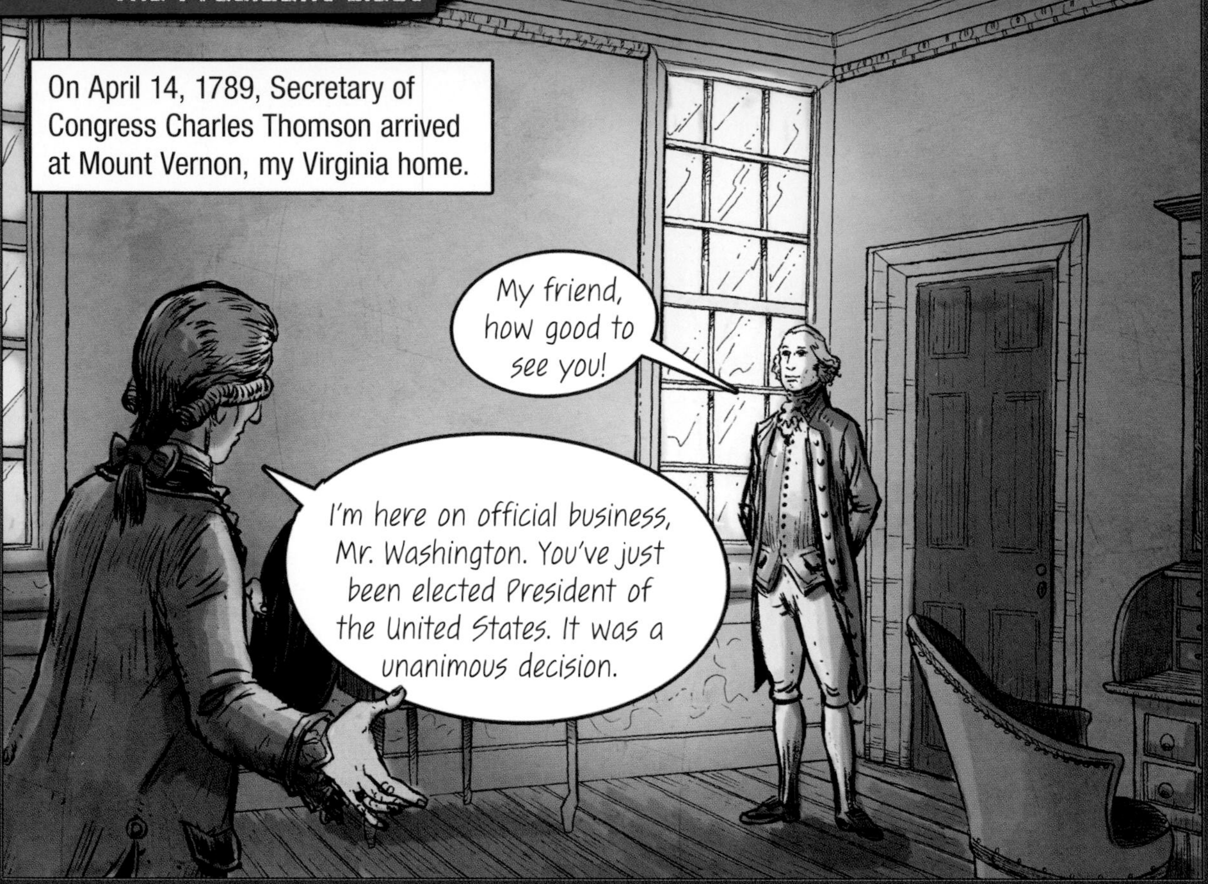
On April 14, 1789, Secretary of Congress Charles Thomson arrived at Mount Vernon, my Virginia home.
My friend, how good to see you!
I'm here on official business, Mr. Washington. You've just been elected President of the United States. It was a unanimous decision.

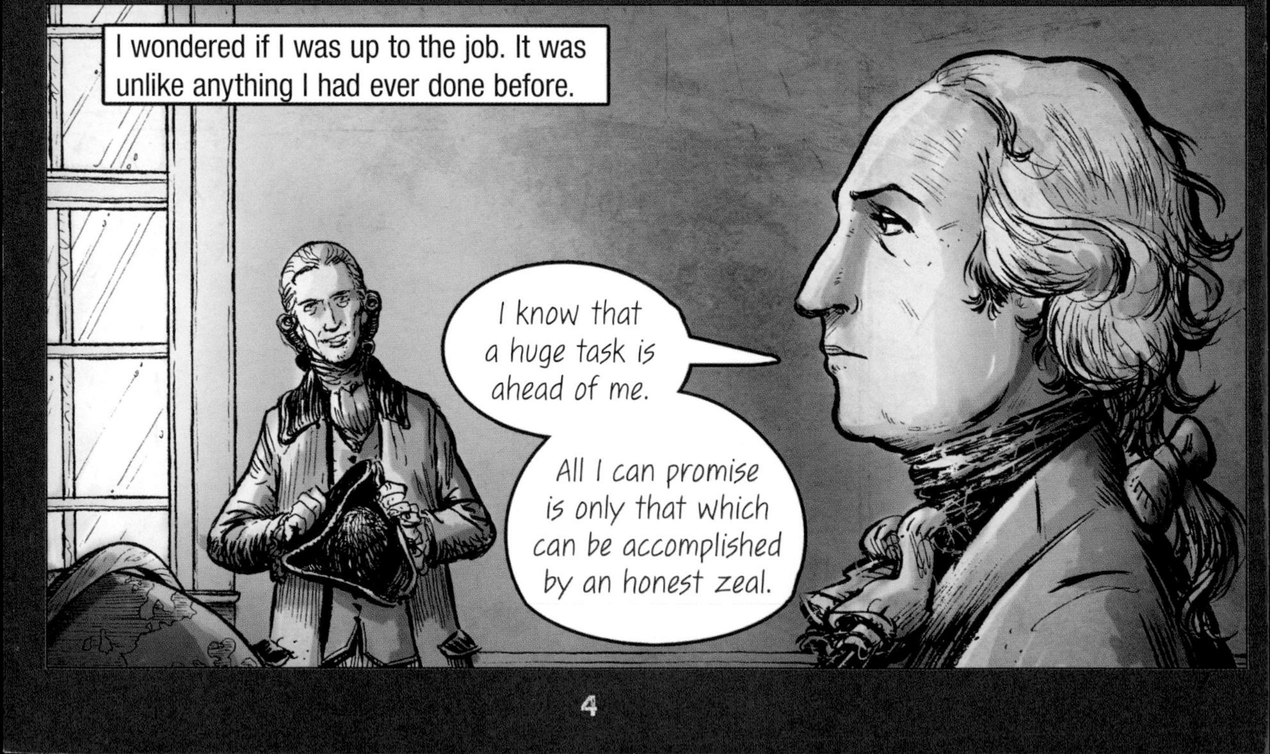
I wondered if I was up to the job. It was unlike anything I had ever done before.
I know that a huge task is ahead of me.
All I can promise is only that which can be accomplished by an honest zeal.

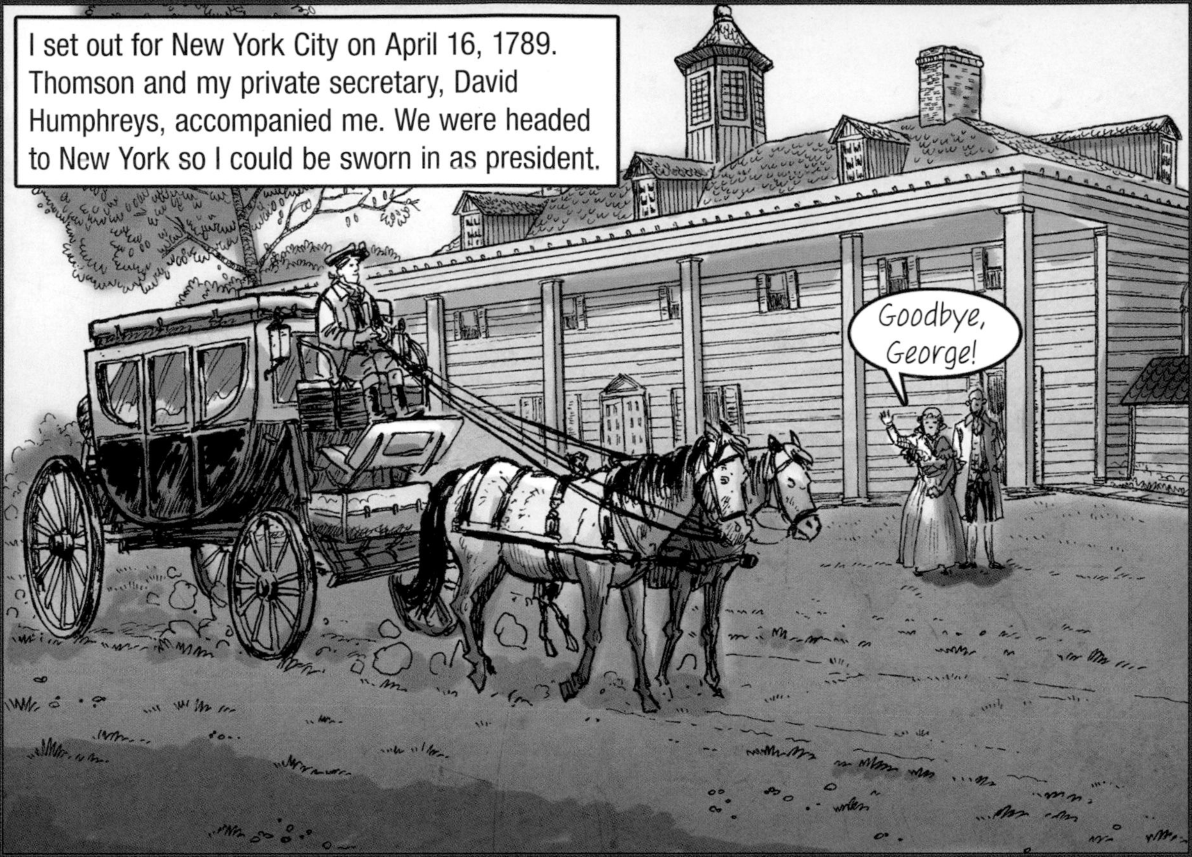
I set out for New York City on April 16, 1789. Thomson and my private secretary, David Humphreys, accompanied me. We were headed to New York so I could be sworn in as president.
Goodbye, George!

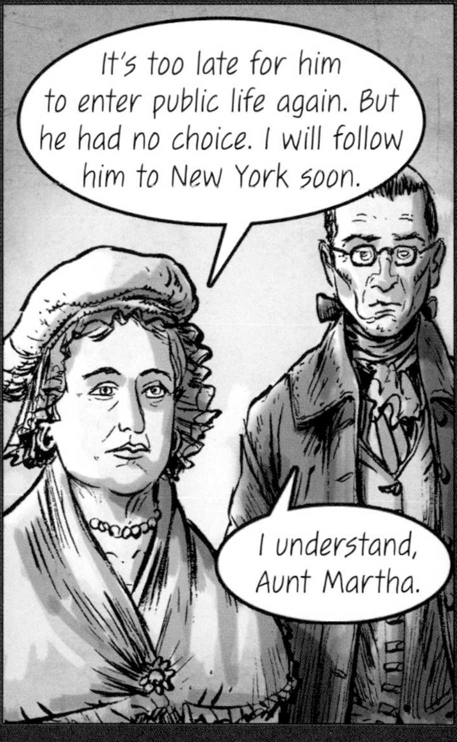
It's too late for him to enter public life again. But he had no choice. I will follow him to New York soon.
I understand, Aunt Martha.

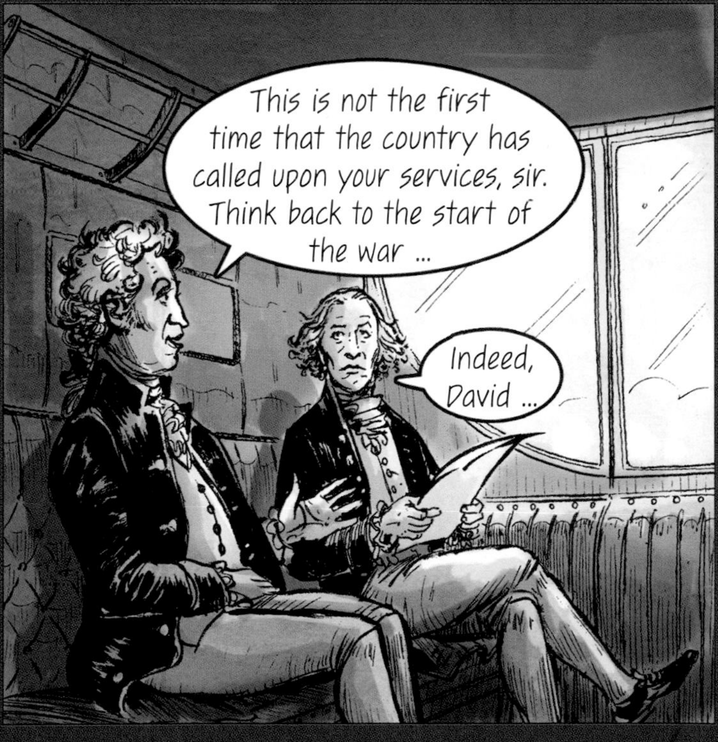
This is not the first time that the country has called upon your services, sir. Think back to the start of the war ...
Indeed, David ...

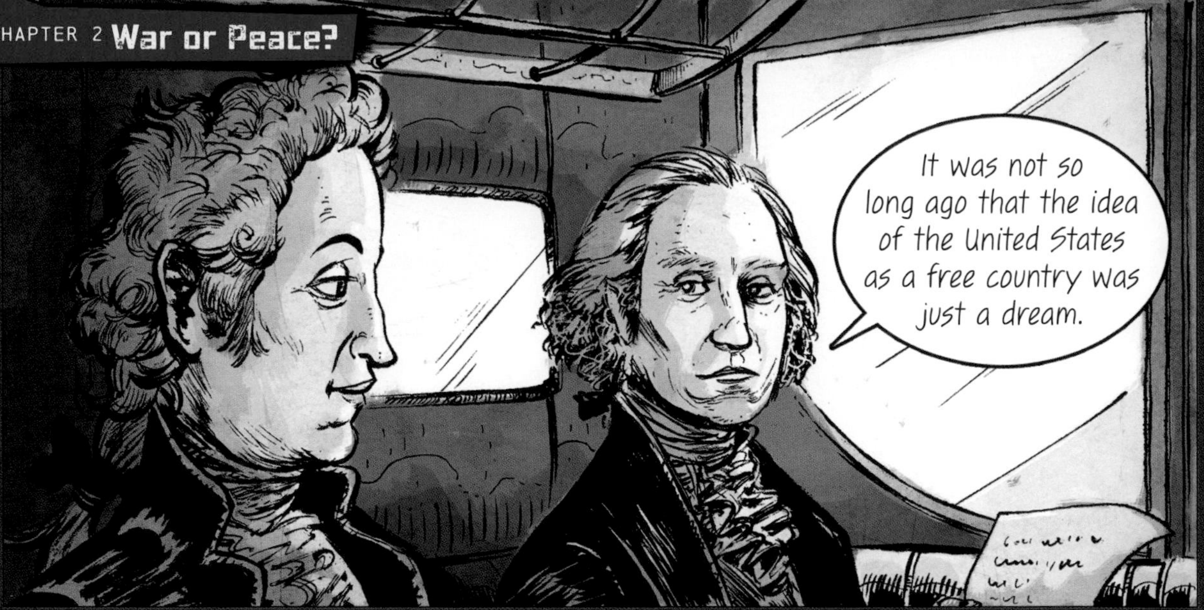
It was not so long ago that the idea of the United States as a free country was just a dream.

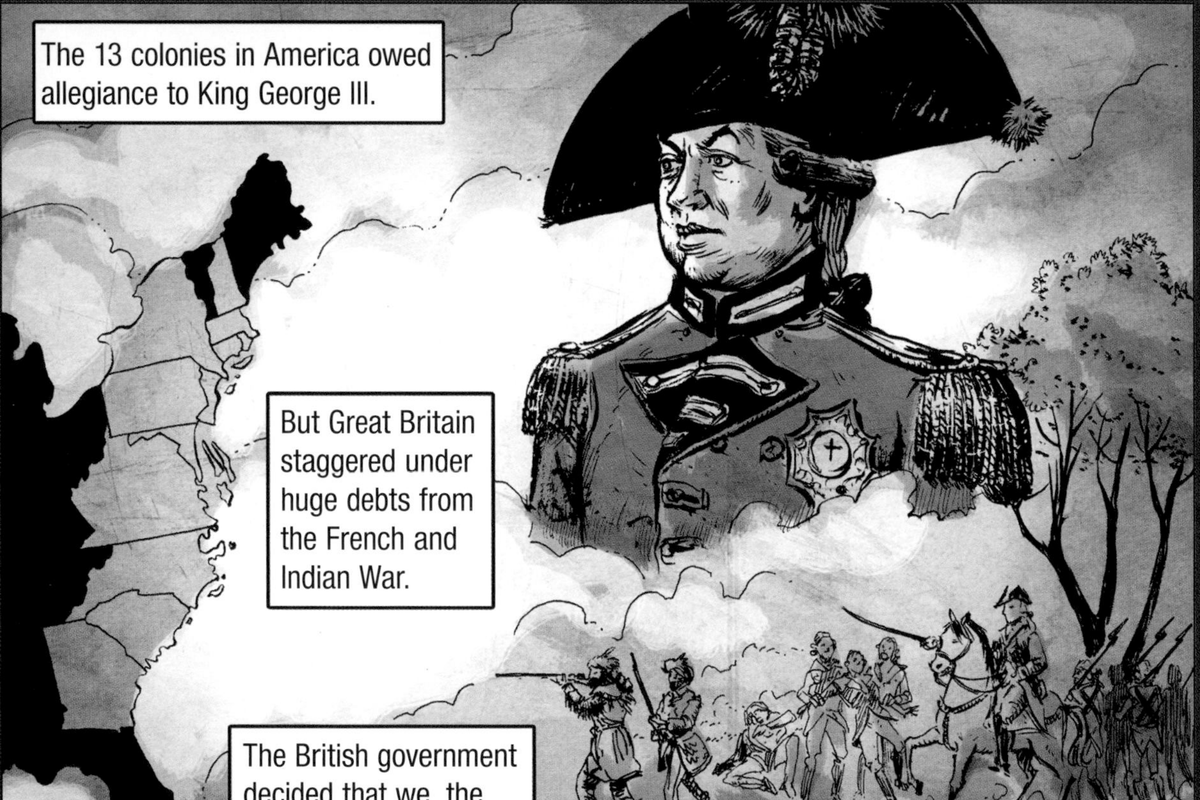
The 13 colonies in America owed allegiance to King George III.
But Great Britain staggered under huge debts from the French and Indian War.
The British government decided that we, the colonists, should pay our share.

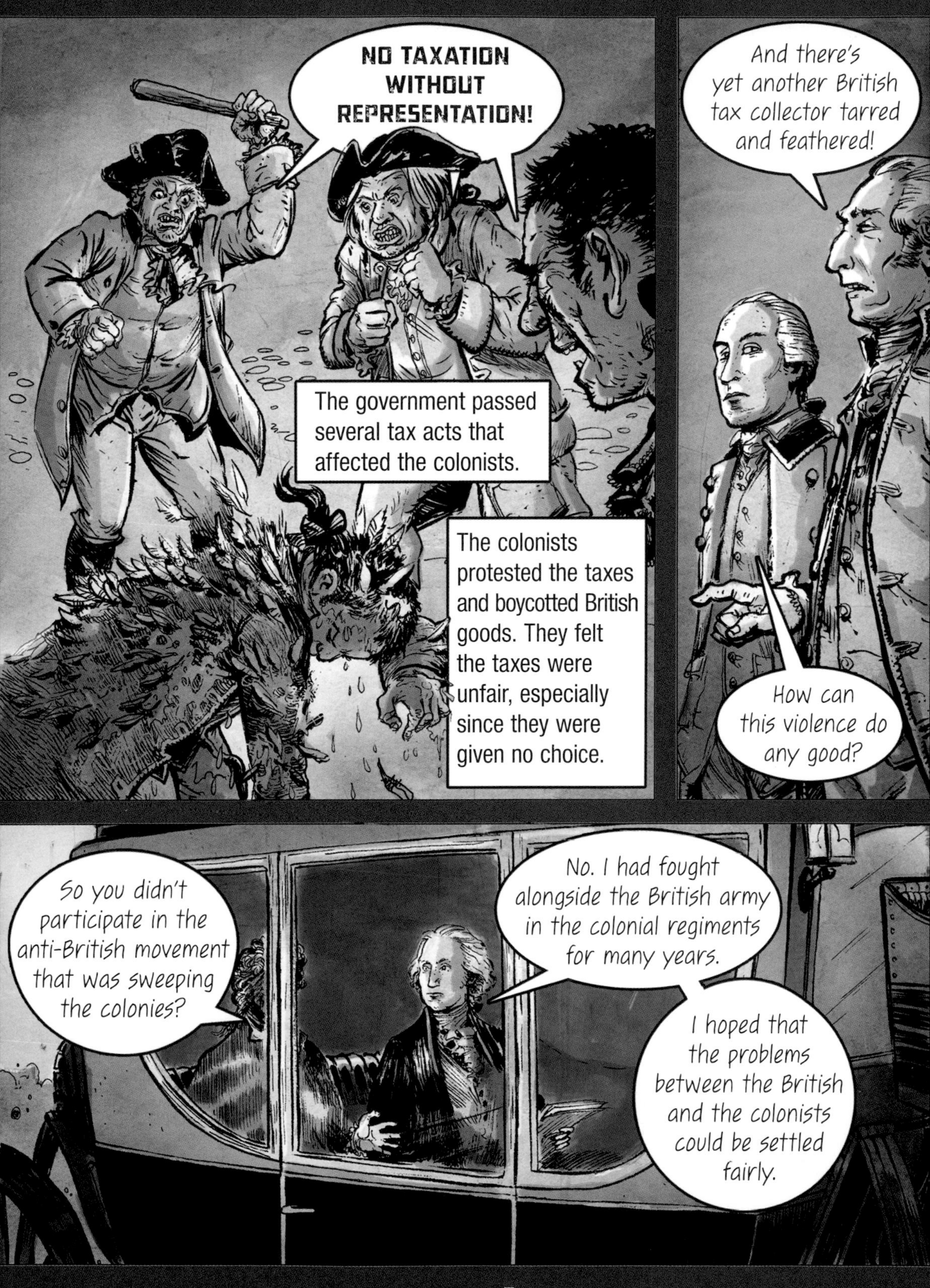
NO TAXATION WITHOUT REPRESENTATION!
The government passed several tax acts that affected the colonists.
The colonists protested the taxes and boycotted British goods. They felt the taxes were unfair, especially since they were given no choice.
And there's yet another British tax collector tarred and feathered!
How can this violence do any good?
So you didn't participate in the anti-British movement that was sweeping the colonies?
No. I had fought alongside the British army in the colonial regiments for many years.
I hoped that the problems between the British and the colonists could be settled fairly.

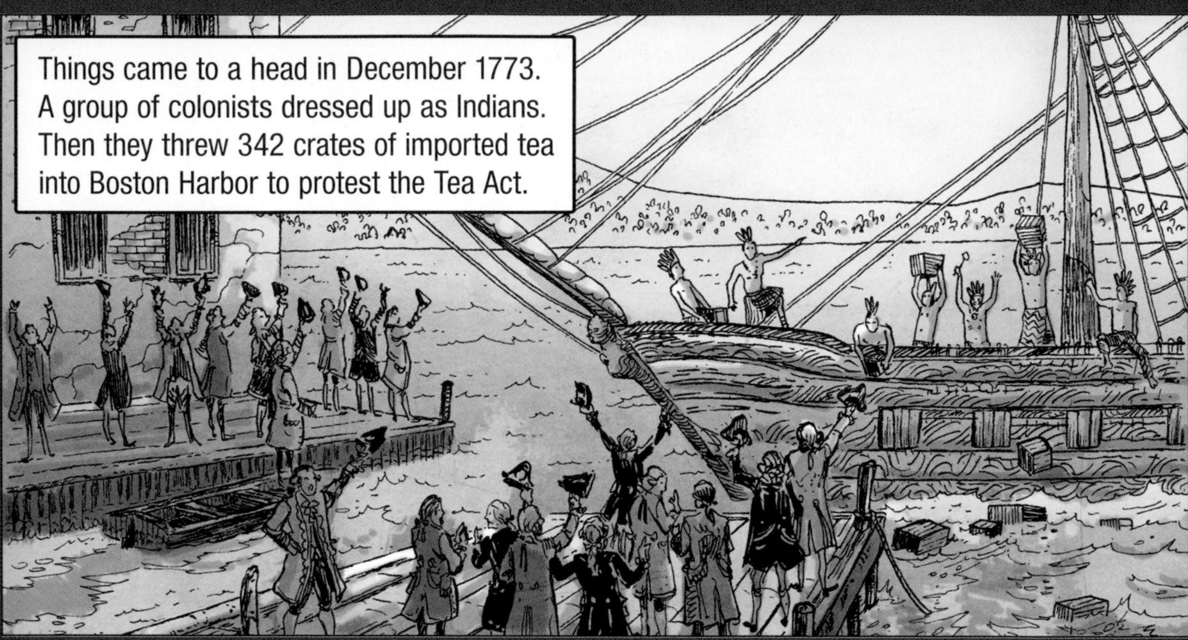
Things came to a head in December 1773. A group of colonists dressed up as Indians. Then they threw 342 crates of imported tea into Boston Harbor to protest the Tea Act.

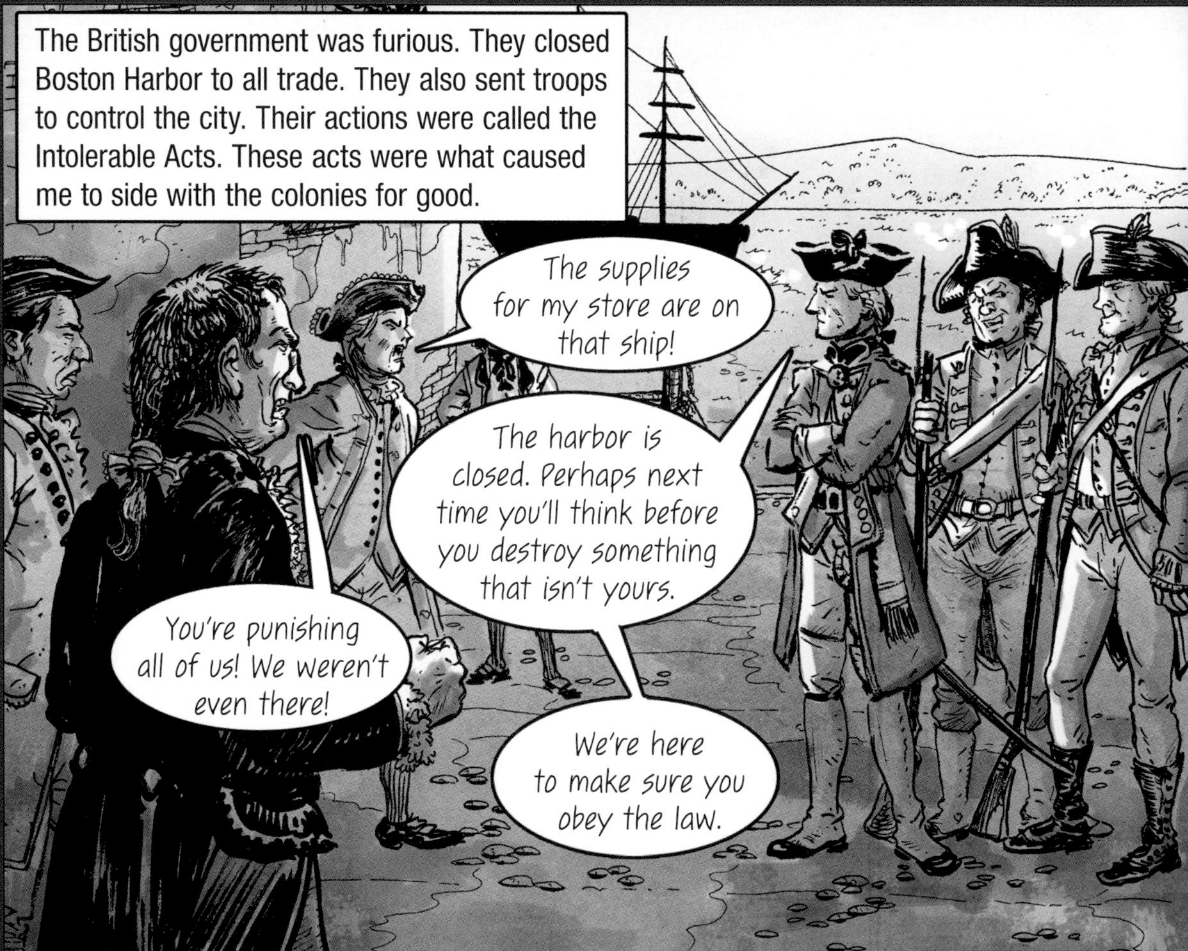
The British government was furious. They closed Boston Harbor to all trade. They also sent troops to control the city. Their actions were called the Intolerable Acts. These acts were what caused me to side with the colonies for good.
The supplies for my store are on that ship!
The harbor is closed. Perhaps next time you'll think before you destroy something that isn't yours.
You're punishing all of us! We weren't even there!
We're here to make sure you obey the law.

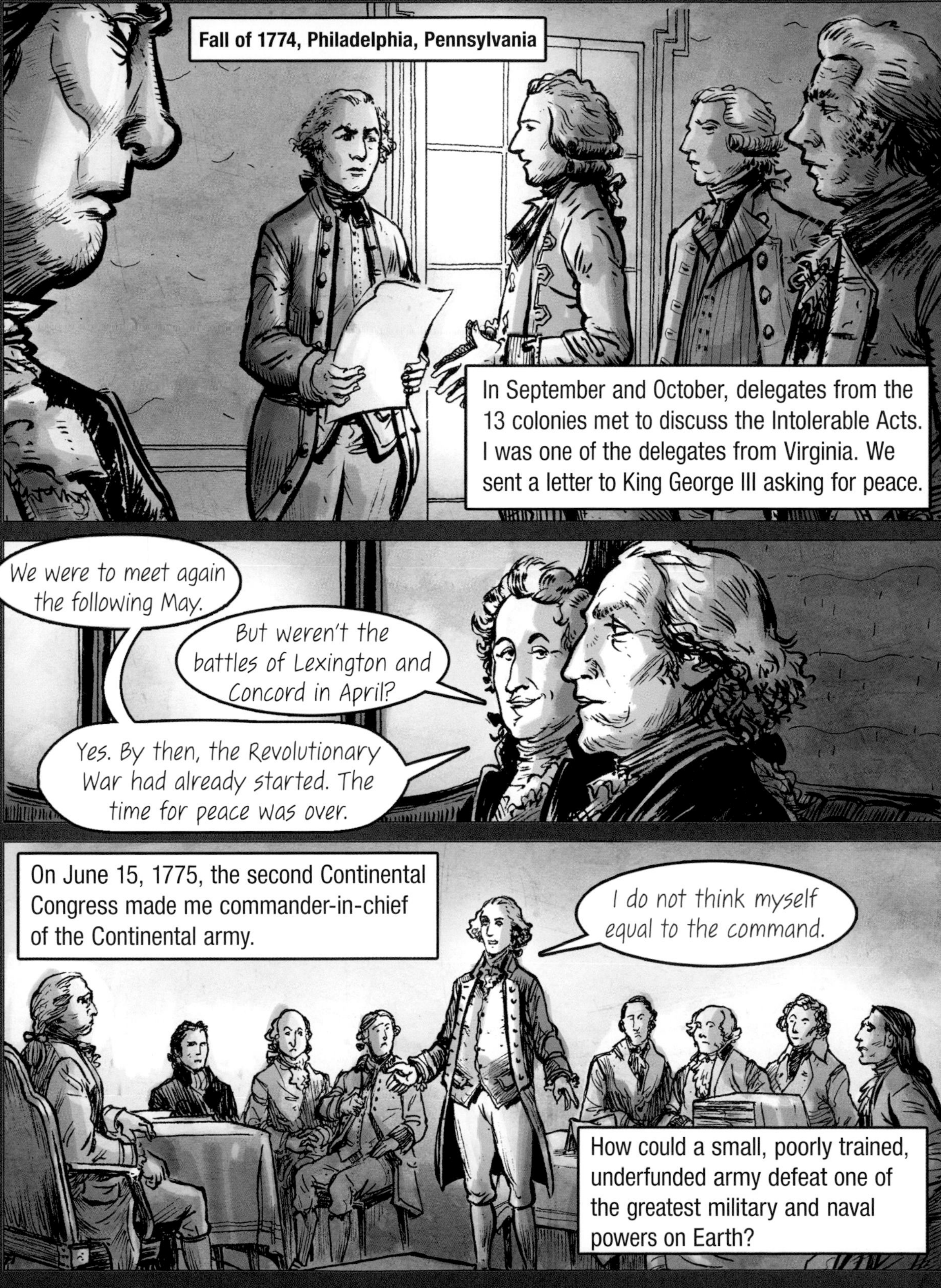
Fall of 1774, Philadelphia, Pennsylvania
In September and October, delegates from the 13 colonies met to discuss the Intolerable Acts. I was one of the delegates from Virginia. We sent a letter to King George III asking for peace.
We were to meet again the following May.
But weren't the battles of Lexington and Concord in April?
Yes. By then, the Revolutionary War had already started. The time for peace was over.
On June 15, 1775, the second Continental Congress made me commander-in-chief of the Continental army.
I do not think myself equal to the command.
How could a small, poorly trained, underfunded army defeat one of the greatest military and naval powers on Earth?

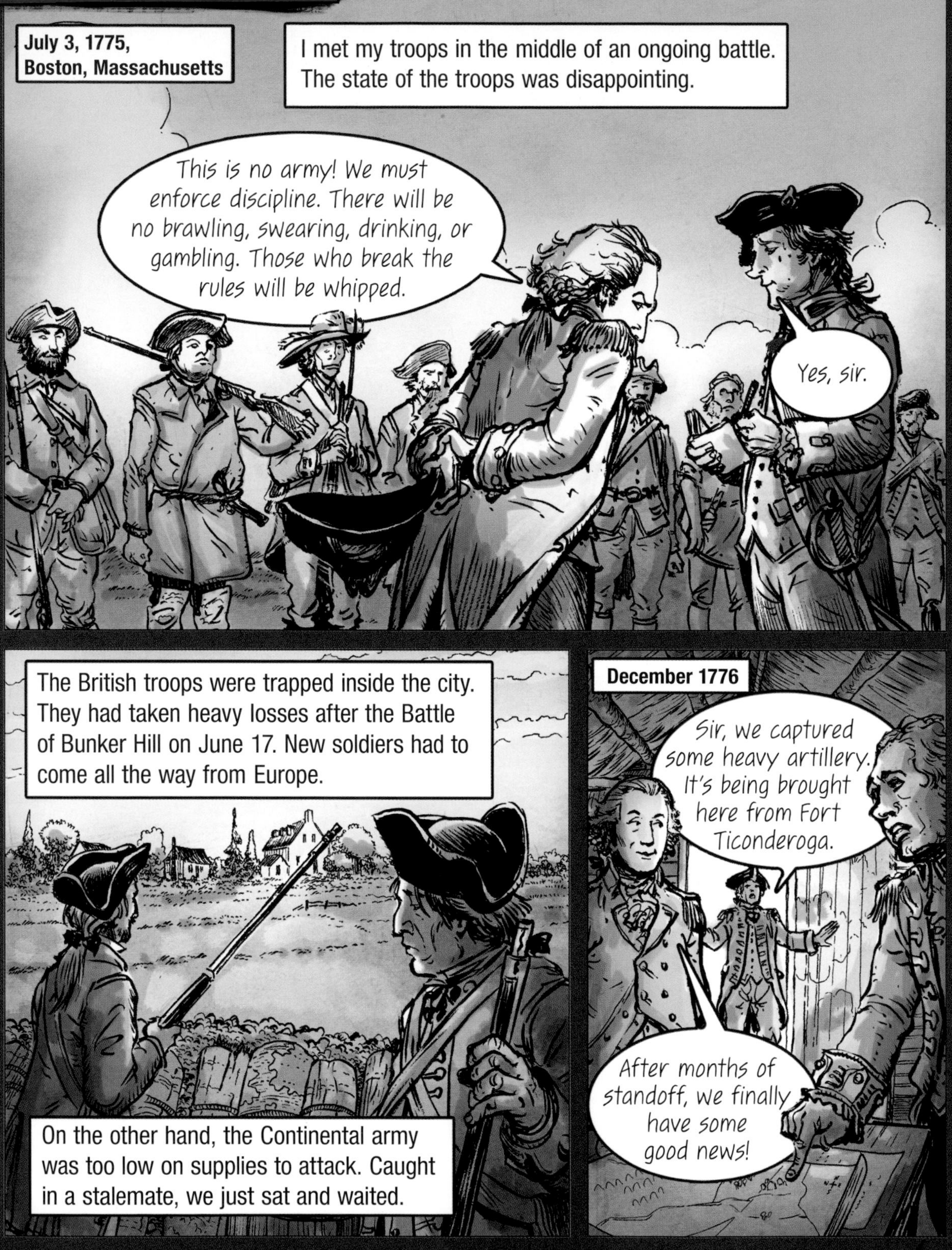
July 3, 1775, Boston, Massachusetts
I met my troops in the middle of an ongoing battle. The state of the troops was disappointing.
This is no army! We must enforce discipline. There will be no brawling, swearing, drinking, or gambling. Those who break the rules will be whipped.
Yes, sir.
The British troops were trapped inside the city. They had taken heavy losses after the Battle of Bunker Hill on June 17. New soldiers had to come all the way from Europe.
On the other hand, the Continental army was too low on supplies to attack. Caught in a stalemate, we just sat and waited.
December 1776
Sir, we captured some heavy artillery. It's being brought here from Fort Ticonderoga.
After months of standoff, we finally have some good news!

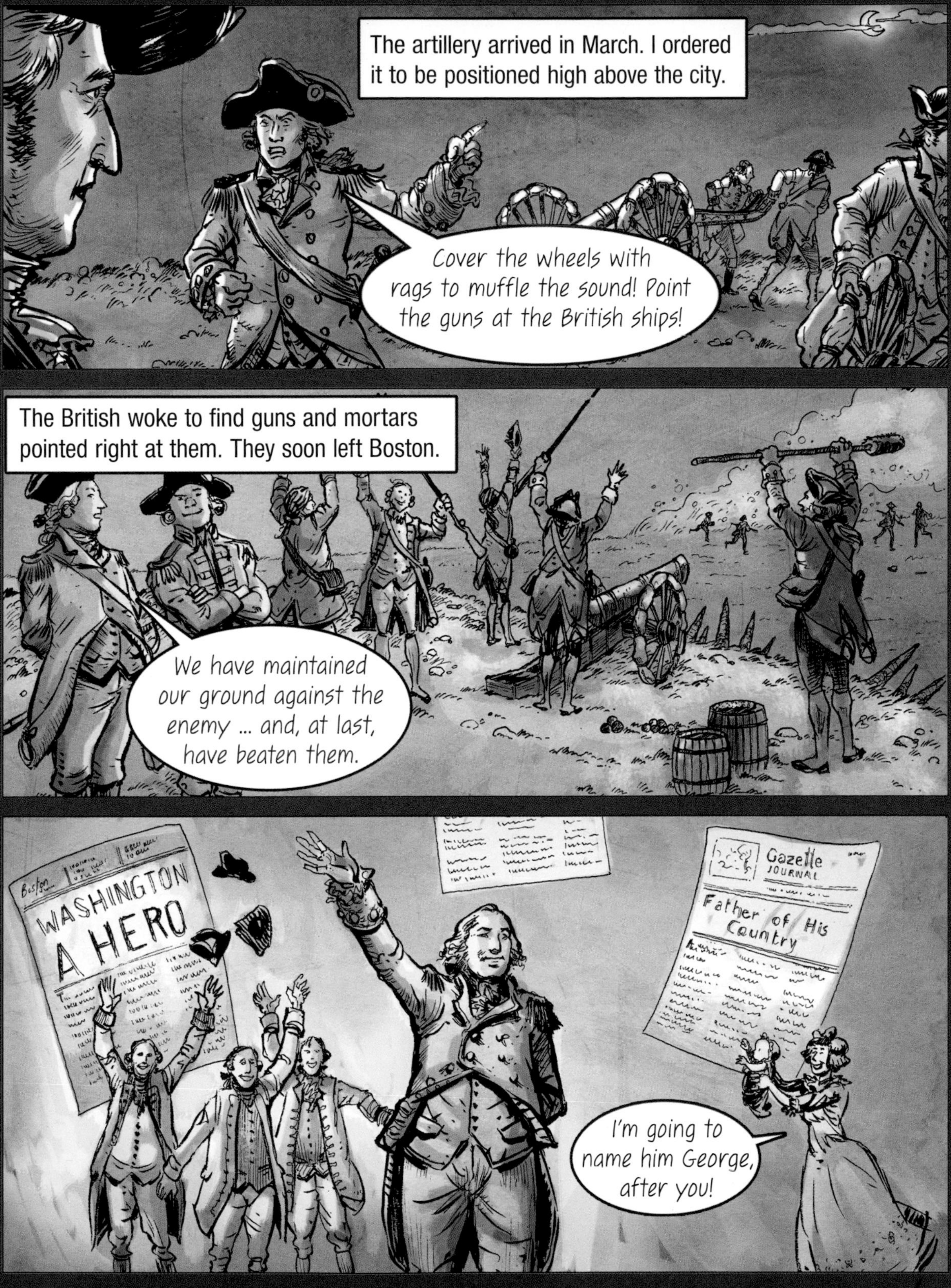
The artillery arrived in March. I ordered it to be positioned high above the city.
Cover the wheels with rags to muffle the sound! Point the guns at the British ships!
The British woke to find guns and mortars pointed right at them. They soon left Boston.
We have maintained our ground against the enemy ... and, at last, have beaten them.
Boston
WASHINGTON A HERO
Gazette JOURNAL
Father of His Country
I'm going to name him George, after you!

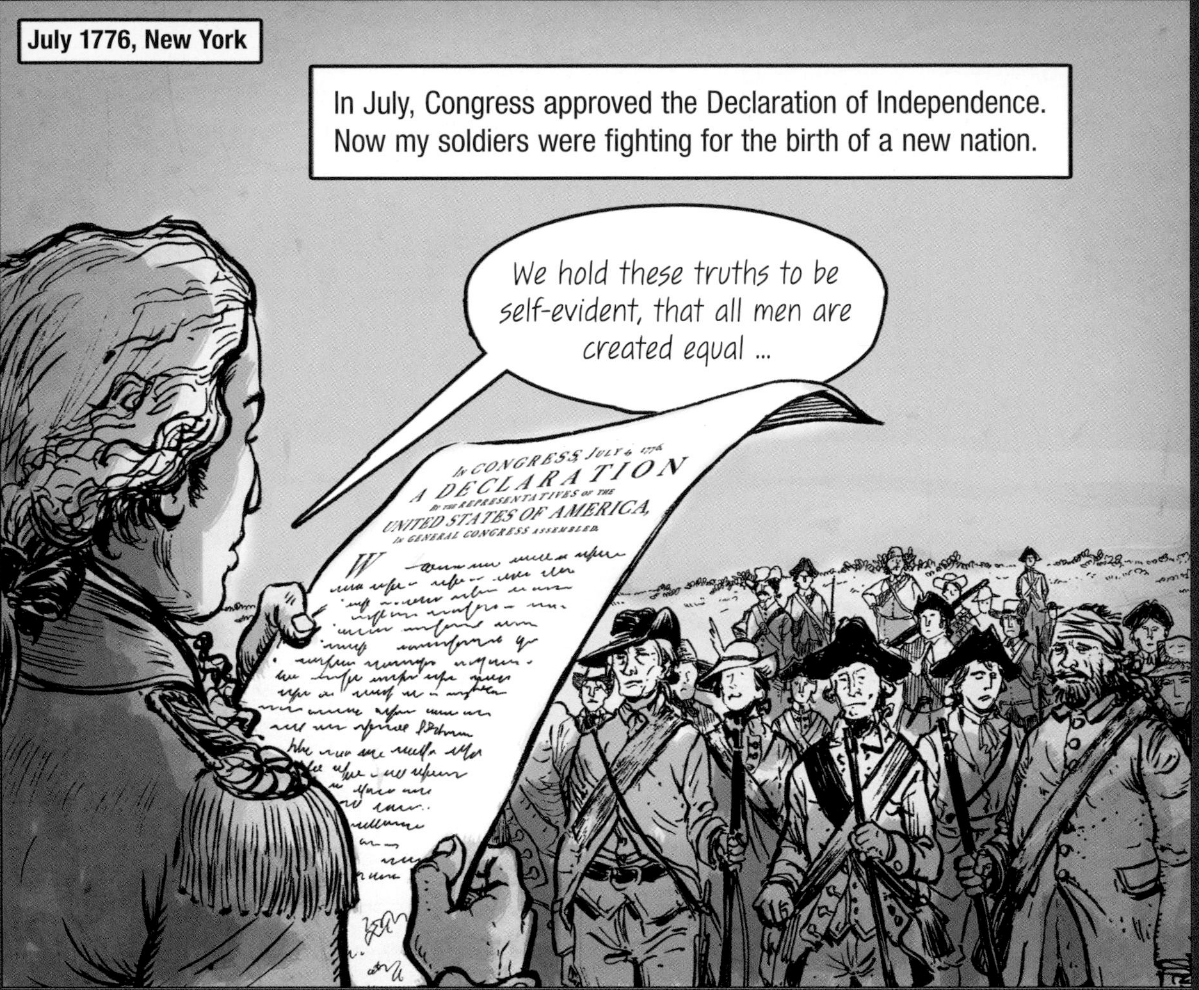
July 1776, New York
In July, Congress approved the Declaration of Independence. Now my soldiers were fighting for the birth of a new nation.
We hold these truths to be self-evident, that all men are created equal ...
IN CONGRESS, JULY 4, 1776.
A DECLARATION
BY THE REPRESENTATIVES OF THE
UNITED STATES OF AMERICA,
IN GENERAL CONGRESS ASSEMBLED.

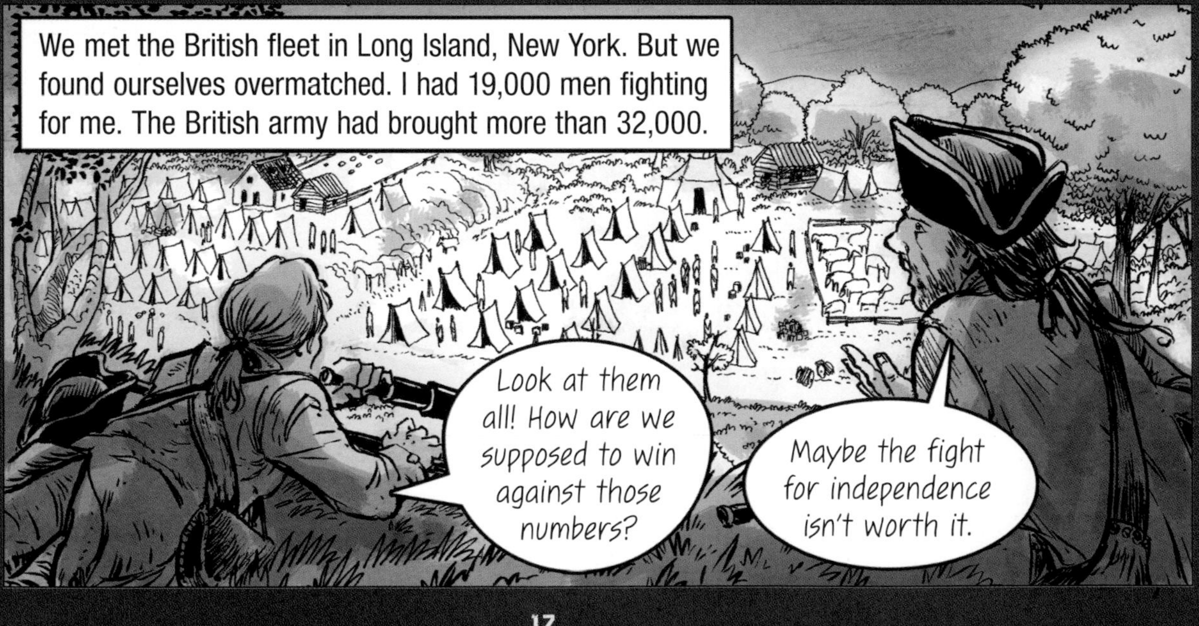
We met the British fleet in Long Island, New York. But we found ourselves overmatched. I had 19,000 men fighting for me. The British army had brought more than 32,000.
Look at them all! How are we supposed to win against those numbers?
Maybe the fight for independence isn't worth it.

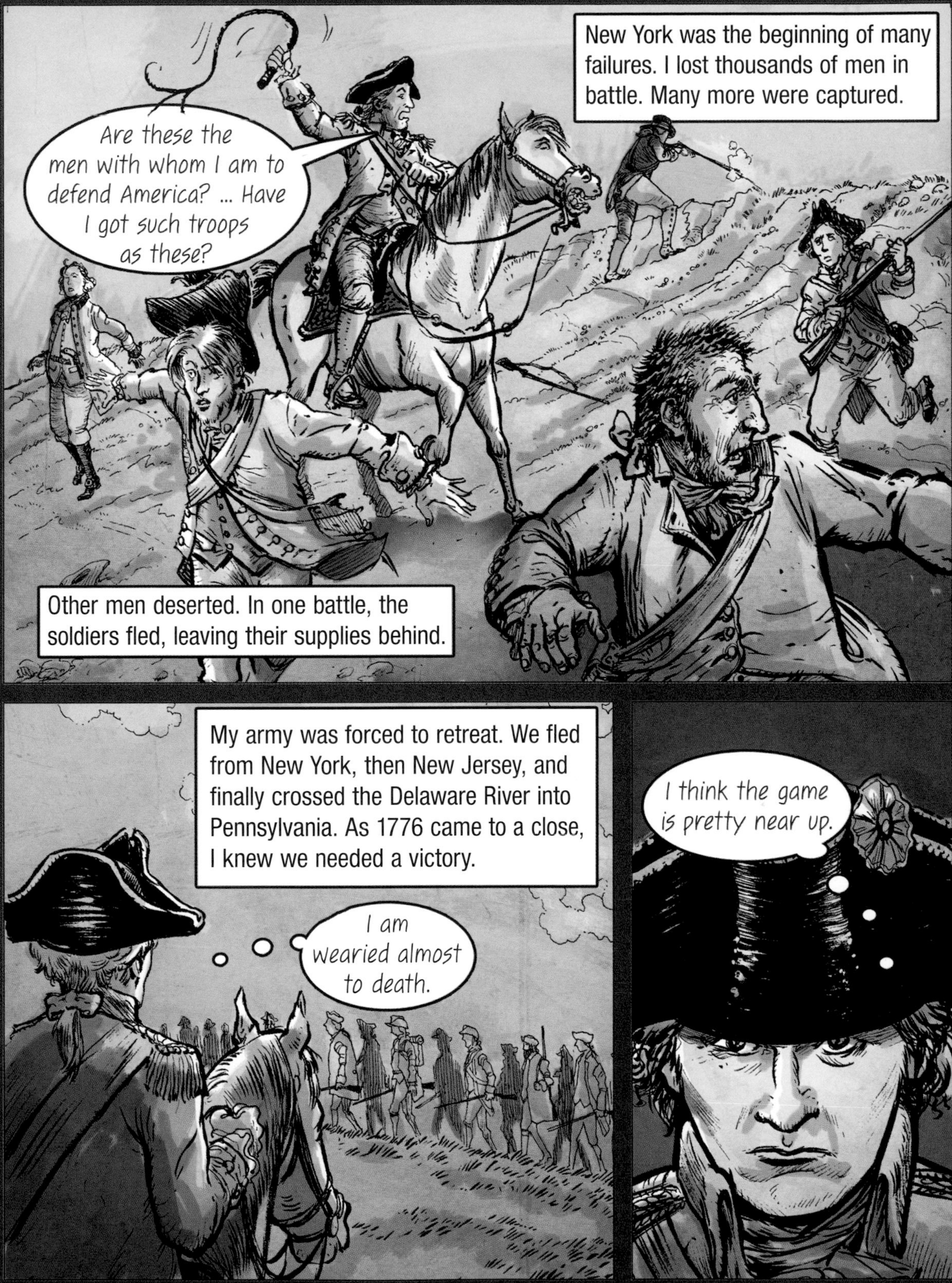
New York was the beginning of many failures. I lost thousands of men in battle. Many more were captured.
Are these the men with whom I am to defend America? ... Have I got such troops as these?
Other men deserted. In one battle, the soldiers fled, leaving their supplies behind.
My army was forced to retreat. We fled from New York, then New Jersey, and finally crossed the Delaware River into Pennsylvania. As 1776 came to a close, I knew we needed a victory.
I am wearied almost to death.
I think the game is pretty near up.

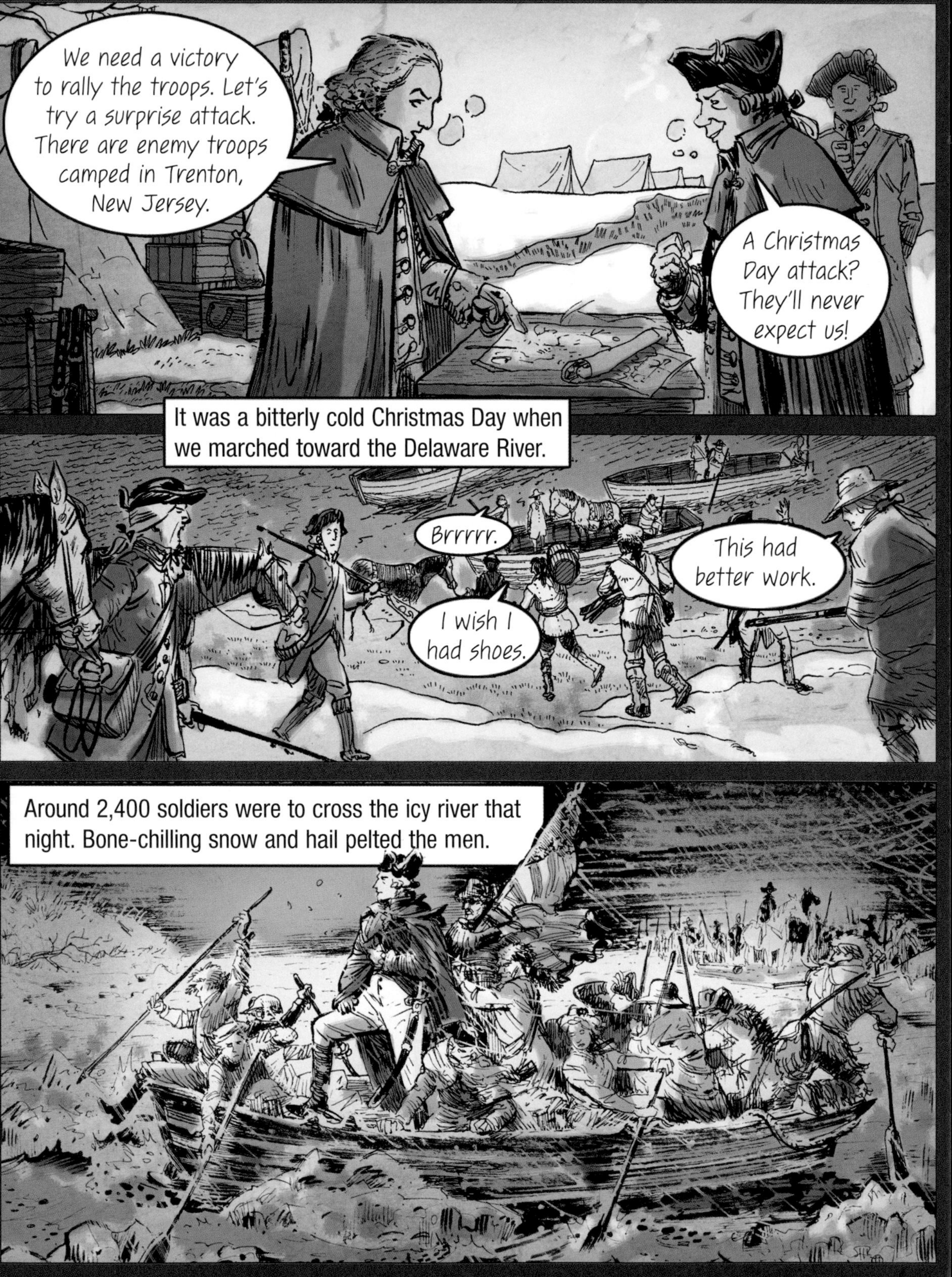
We need a victory to rally the troops. Let's try a surprise attack. There are enemy troops camped in Trenton, New Jersey.
A Christmas Day attack? They'll never expect us!
It was a bitterly cold Christmas Day when we marched toward the Delaware River.
Brrrrr.
I wish I had shoes.
This had better work.
Around 2,400 soldiers were to cross the icy river that night. Bone-chilling snow and hail pelted the men.

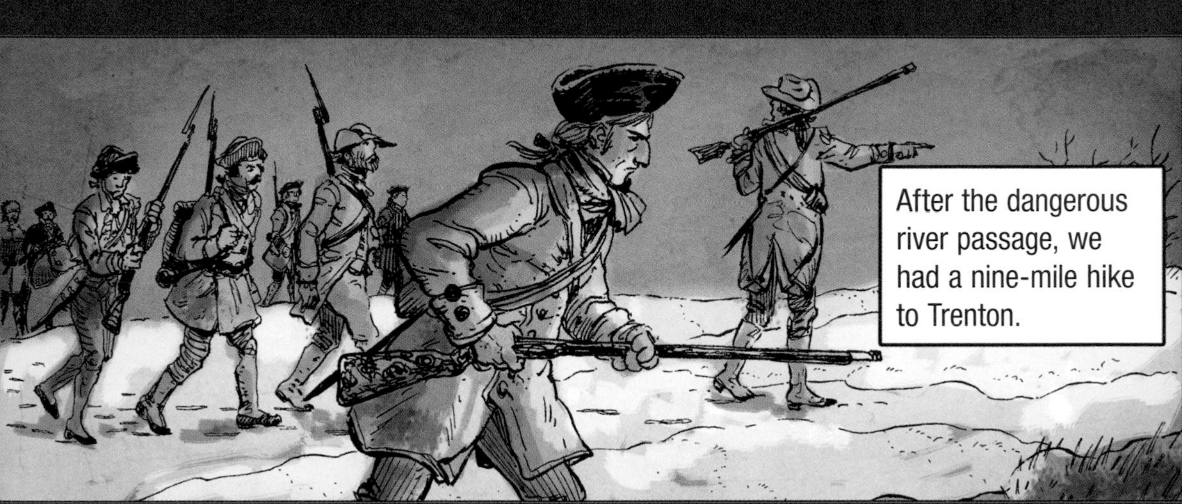
After the dangerous river passage, we had a nine-mile hike to Trenton.

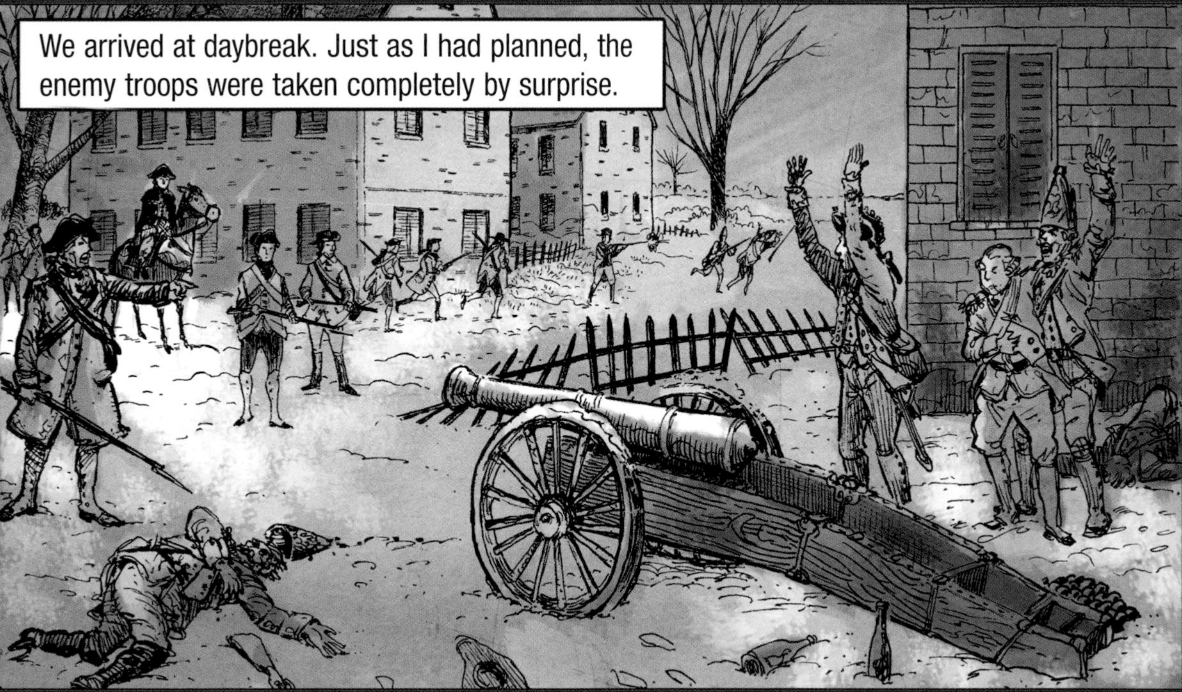
We arrived at daybreak. Just as I had planned, the enemy troops were taken completely by surprise.

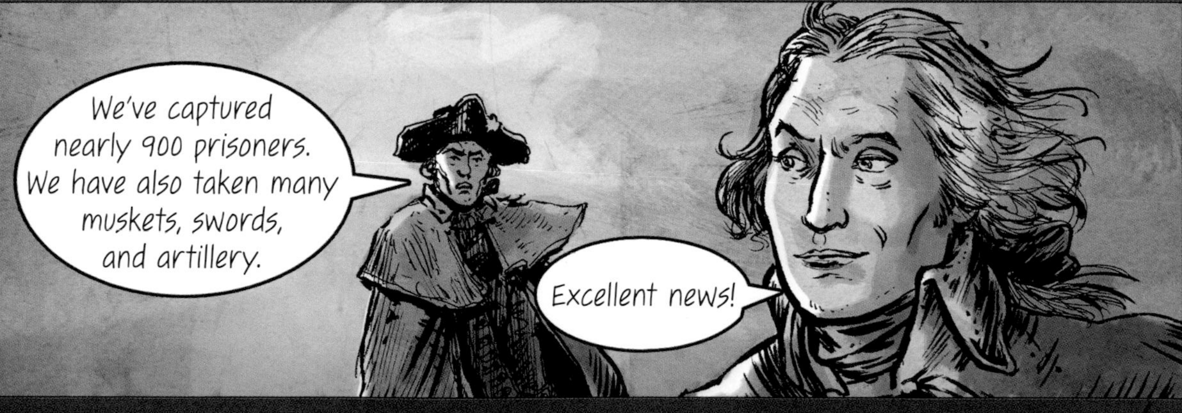
We've captured nearly 900 prisoners. We have also taken many muskets, swords, and artillery.
Excellent news!

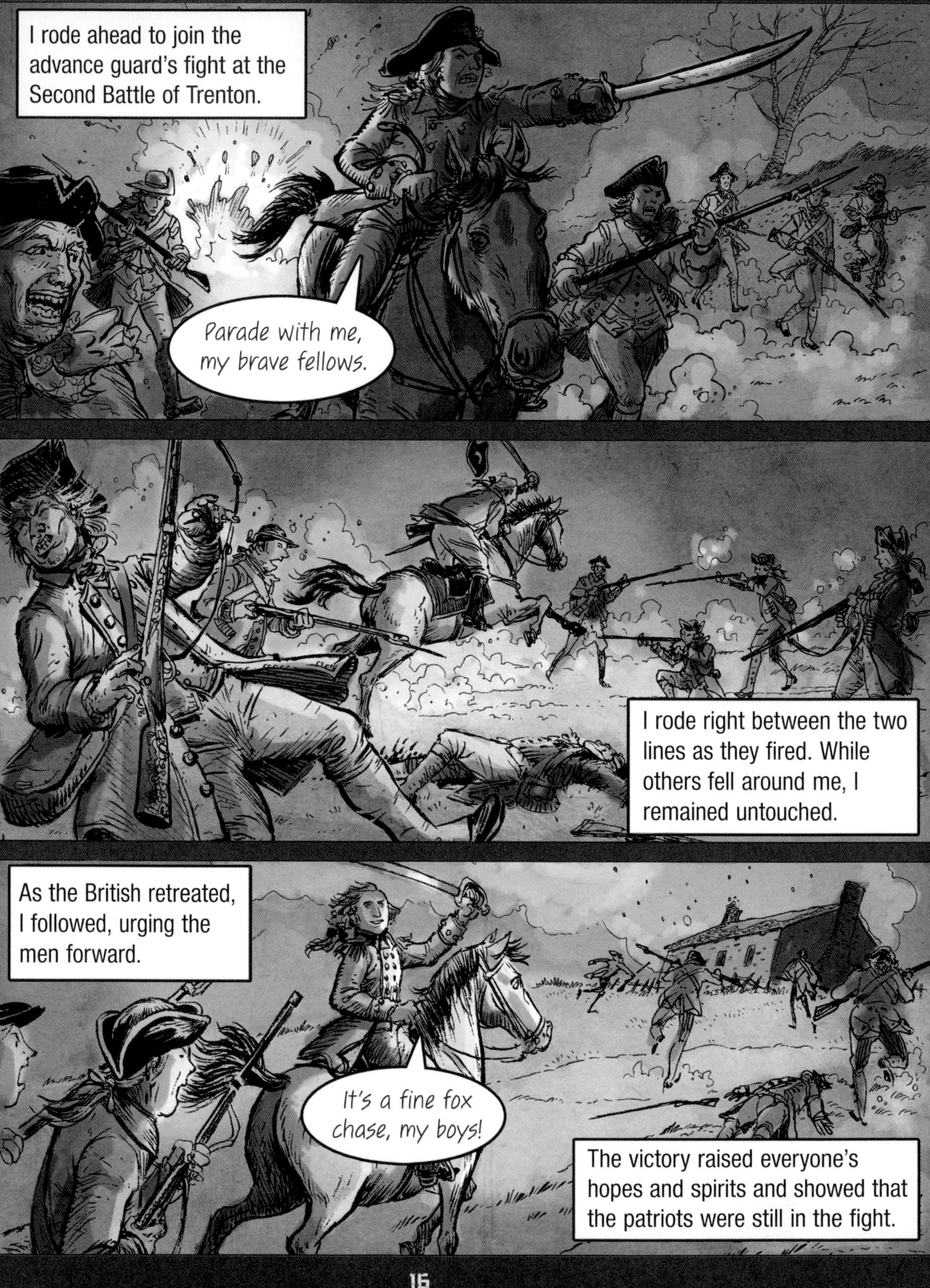
I rode ahead to join the advance guard's fight at the Second Battle of Trenton.
Parade with me, my brave fellows.
I rode right between the two lines as they fired. While others fell around me, I remained untouched.
As the British retreated, I followed, urging the men forward.
It's a fine fox chase, my boys!
The victory raised everyone's hopes and spirits and showed that the patriots were still in the fight.

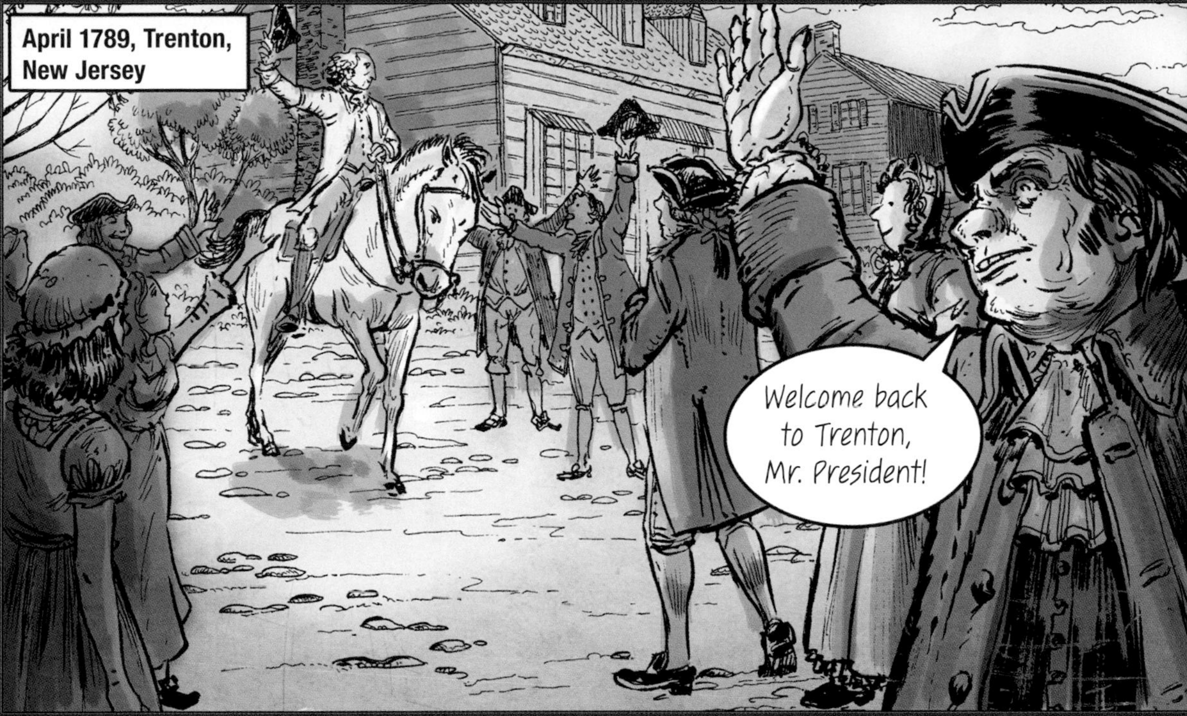
April 1789, Trenton, New Jersey
Welcome back to Trenton, Mr. President!

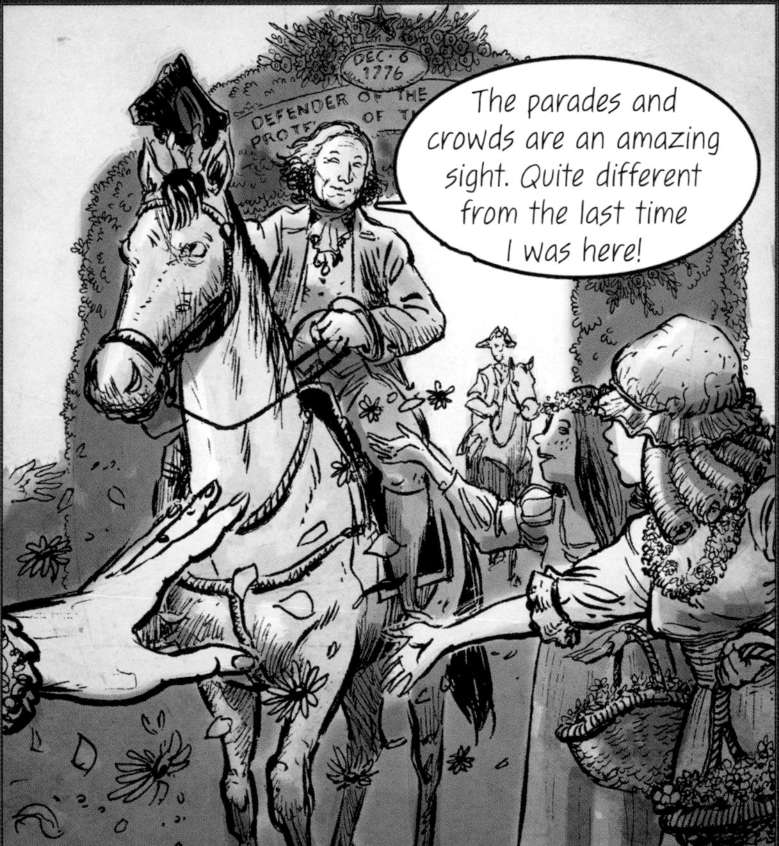
DEC. 6 1776
DEFENDER OF THE
The parades and crowds are an amazing sight. Quite different from the last time I was here!

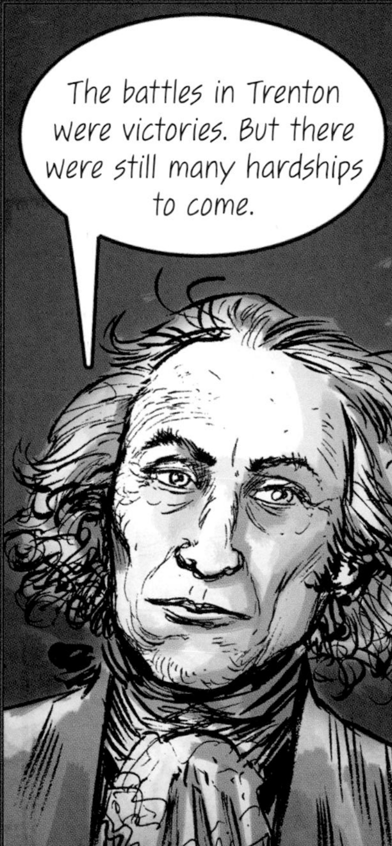
The battles in Trenton were victories. But there were still many hardships to come.

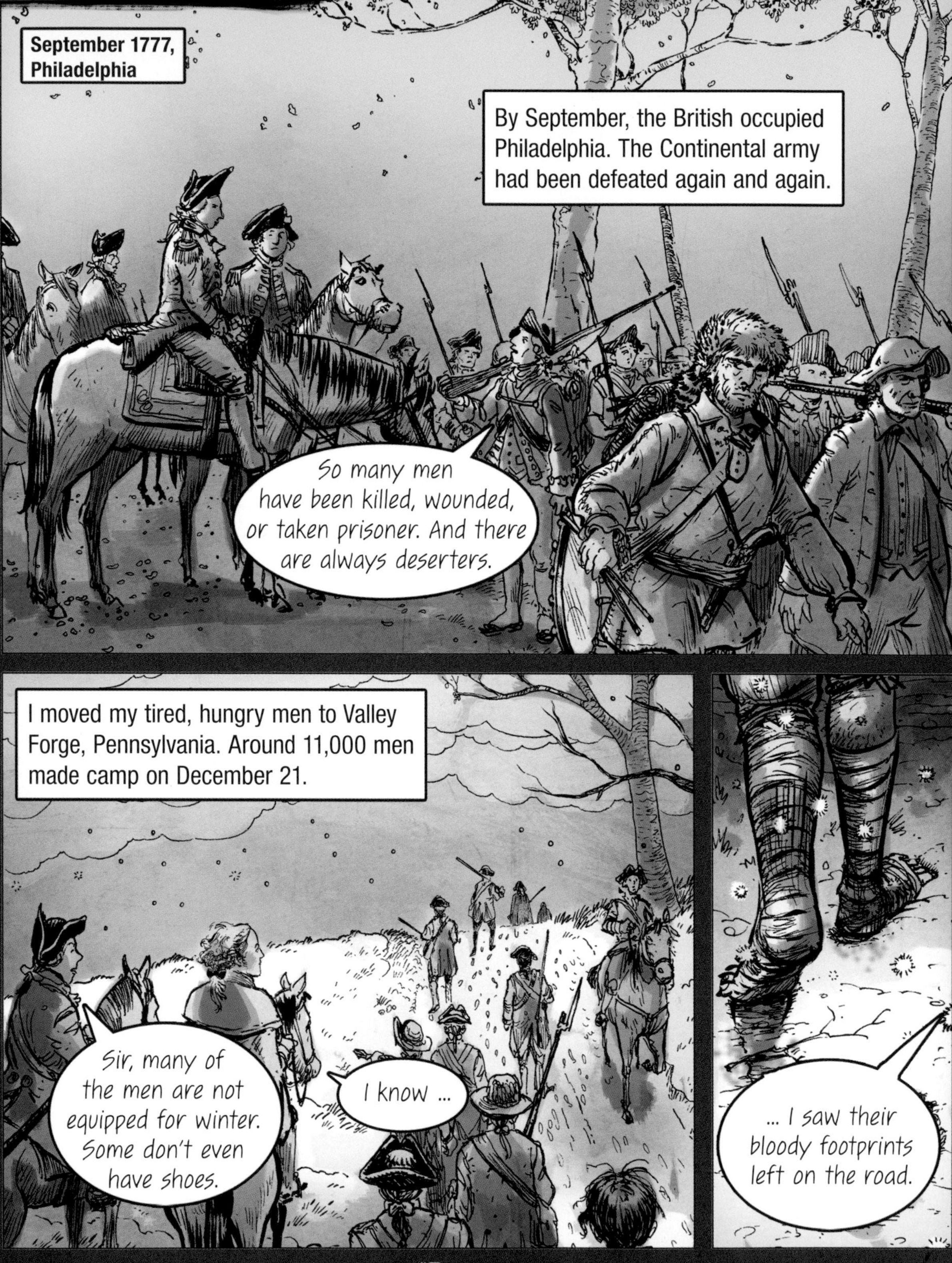
September 1777, Philadelphia
By September, the British occupied Philadelphia. The Continental army had been defeated again and again.
So many men have been killed, wounded, or taken prisoner. And there are always deserters.
I moved my tired, hungry men to Valley Forge, Pennsylvania. Around 11,000 men made camp on December 21.
Sir, many of the men are not equipped for winter. Some don't even have shoes.
I know ...
... I saw their bloody footprints left on the road.

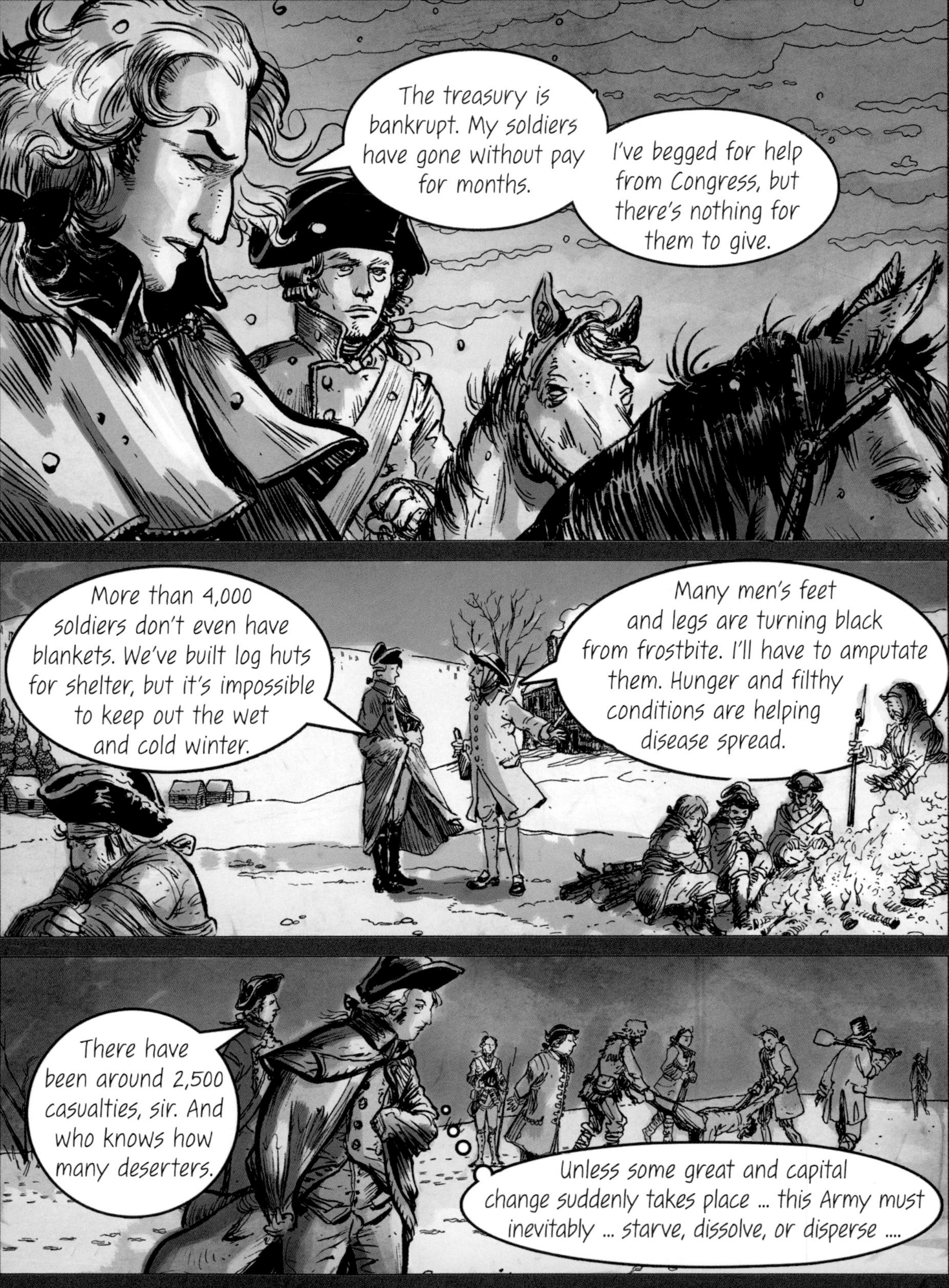
The treasury is bankrupt. My soldiers have gone without pay for months.
I've begged for help from Congress, but there's nothing for them to give.
More than 4,000 soldiers don't even have blankets. We've built log huts for shelter, but it's impossible to keep out the wet and cold winter.
Many men's feet and legs are turning black from frostbite. I'll have to amputate them. Hunger and filthy conditions are helping disease spread.
There have been around 2,500 casualties, sir. And who knows how many deserters.
Unless some great and capital change suddenly takes place ... this Army must inevitably ... starve, dissolve, or disperse ....

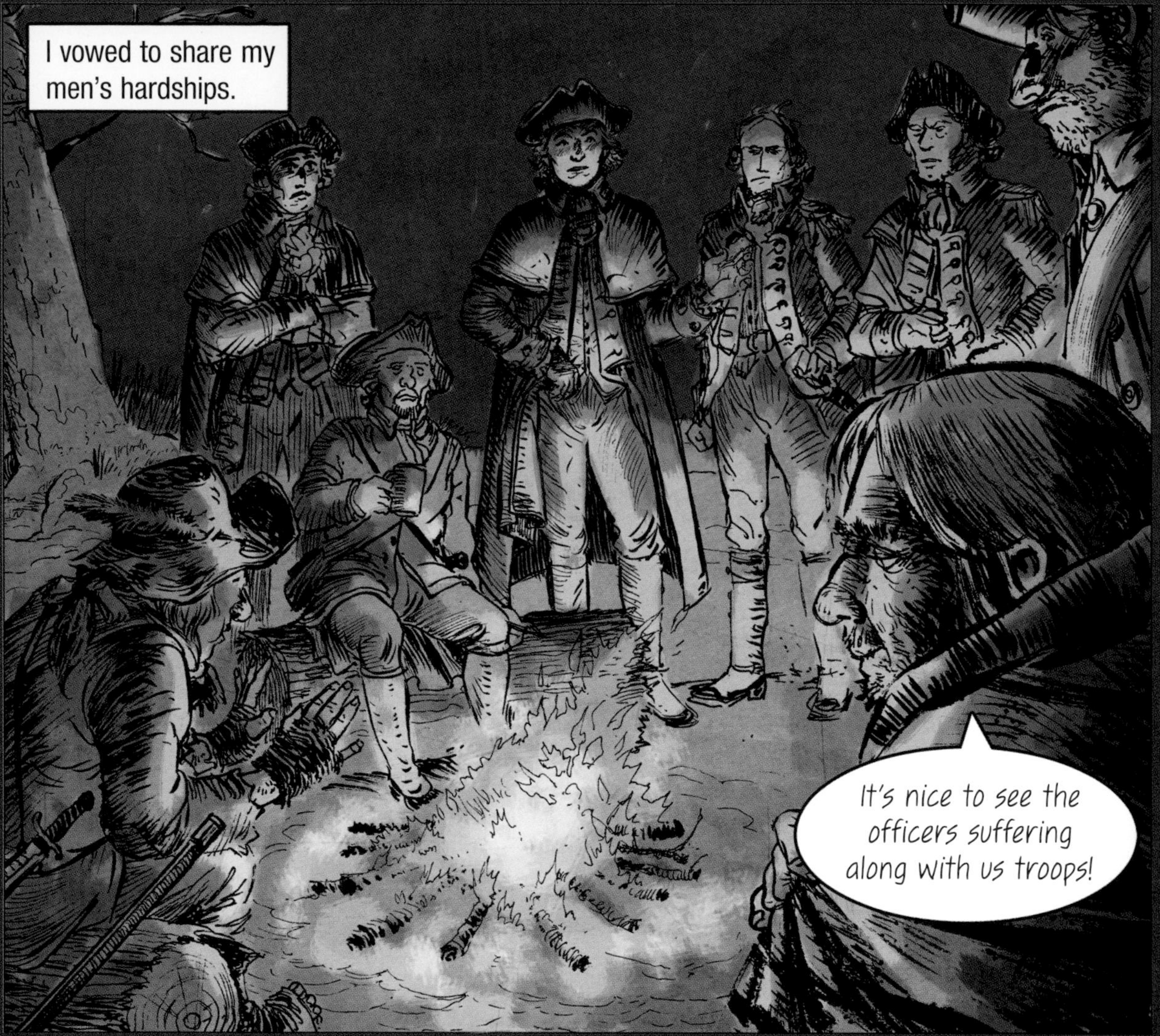
I vowed to share my men's hardships.
It's nice to see the officers suffering along with us troops!

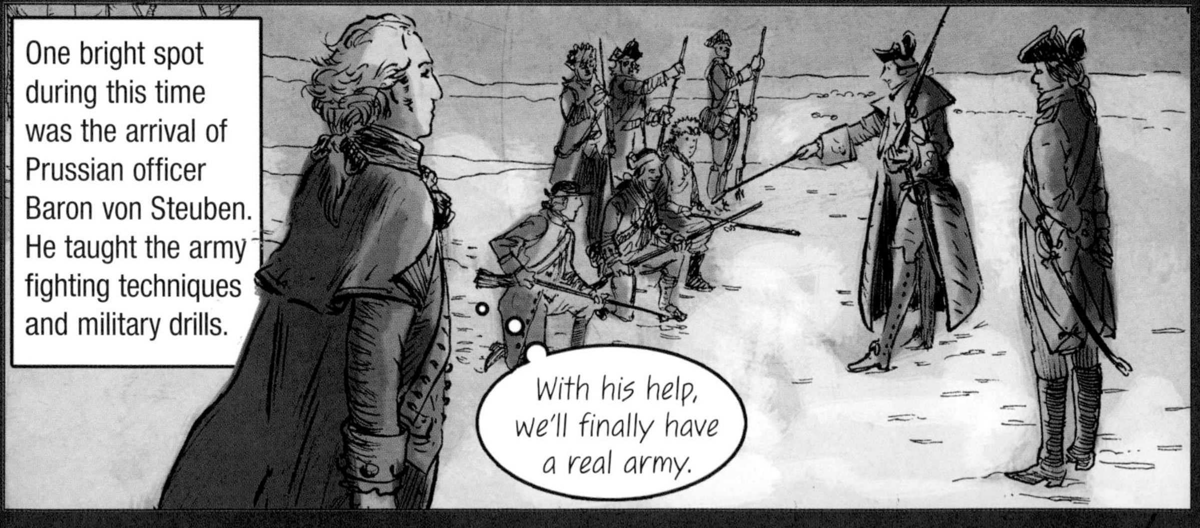
One bright spot during this time was the arrival of Prussian officer Baron von Steuben. He taught the army fighting techniques and military drills.
With his help, we'll finally have a real army.

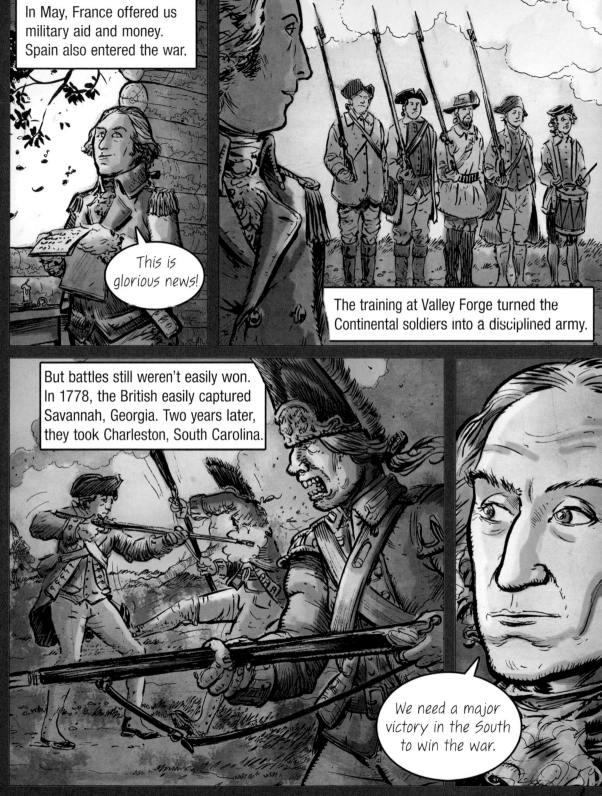

In May, France offered us military aid and money. Spain also entered the war.

This is glorious news!

The training at Valley Forge turned the Continental soldiers into a disciplined army.

But battles still weren't easily won. In 1778, the British easily captured Savannah, Georgia. Two years later, they took Charleston, South Carolina.

We need a major victory in the South to win the war.

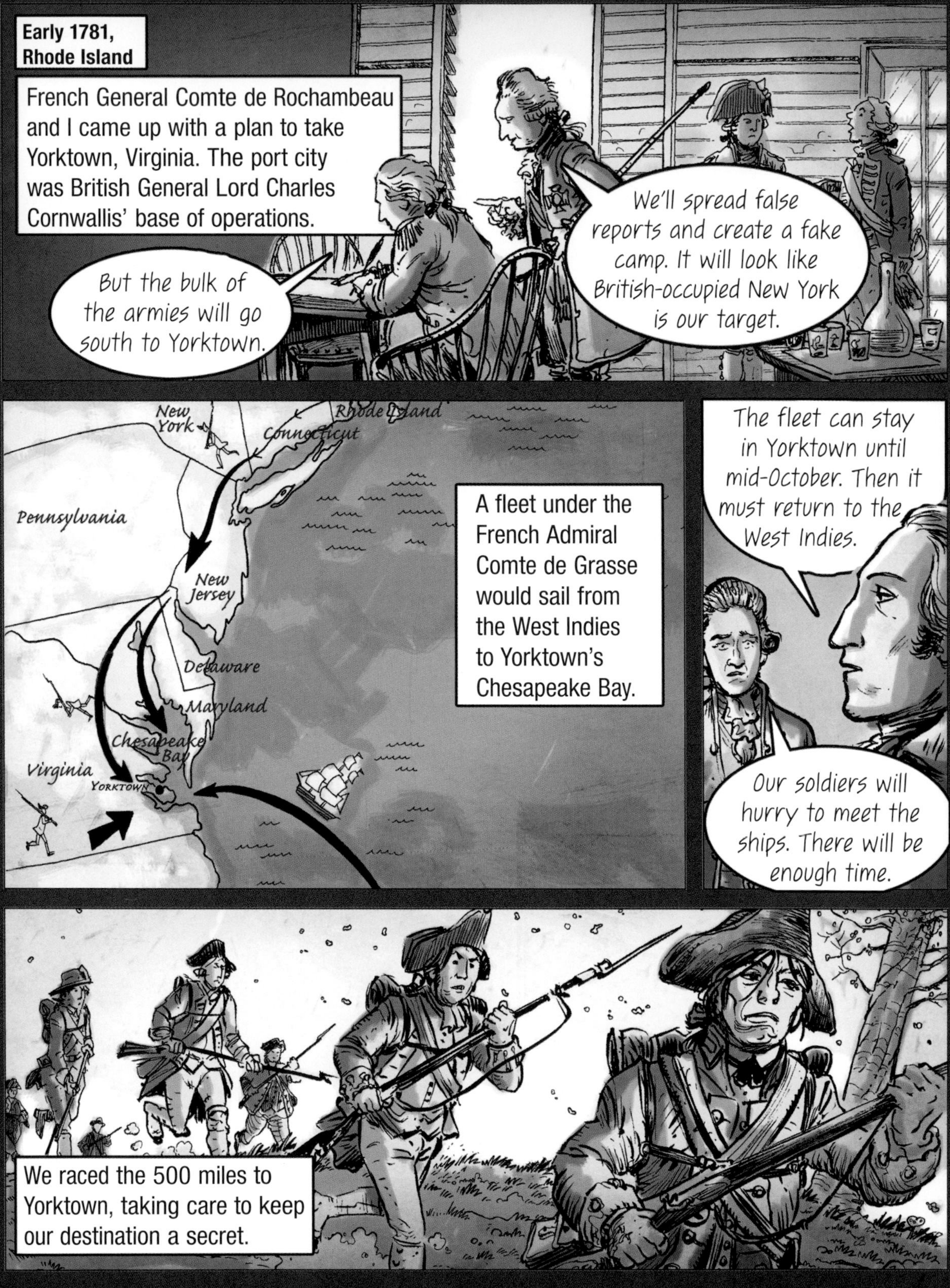
Early 1781, Rhode Island
French General Comte de Rochambeau and I came up with a plan to take Yorktown, Virginia. The port city was British General Lord Charles Cornwallis' base of operations.
We'll spread false reports and create a fake camp. It will look like British-occupied New York is our target.
But the bulk of the armies will go south to Yorktown.
New York
Rhode Island
Connecticut
Pennsylvania
New Jersey
Delaware
Maryland
Chesapeake Bay
Virginia
YORKTOWN
A fleet under the French Admiral Comte de Grasse would sail from the West Indies to Yorktown's Chesapeake Bay.
The fleet can stay in Yorktown until mid-October. Then it must return to the West Indies.
Our soldiers will hurry to meet the ships. There will be enough time.
We raced the 500 miles to Yorktown, taking care to keep our destination a secret.

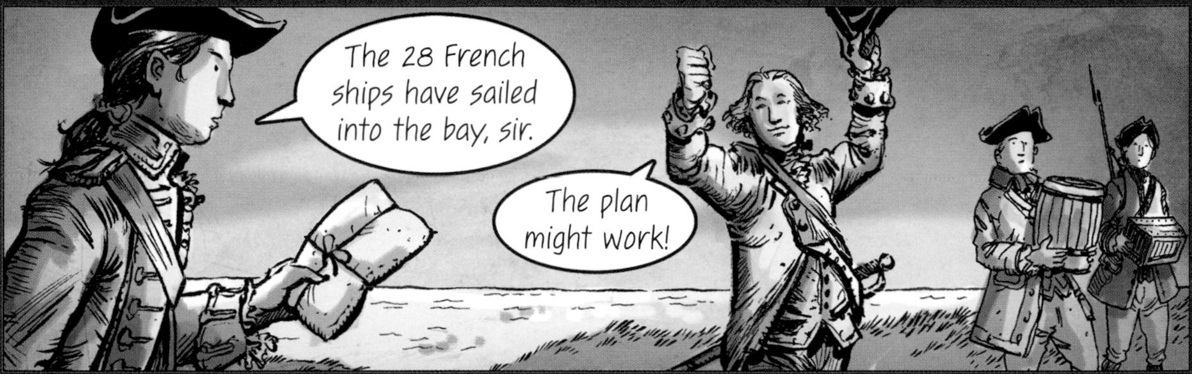
The 28 French ships have sailed into the bay, sir.
The plan might work!

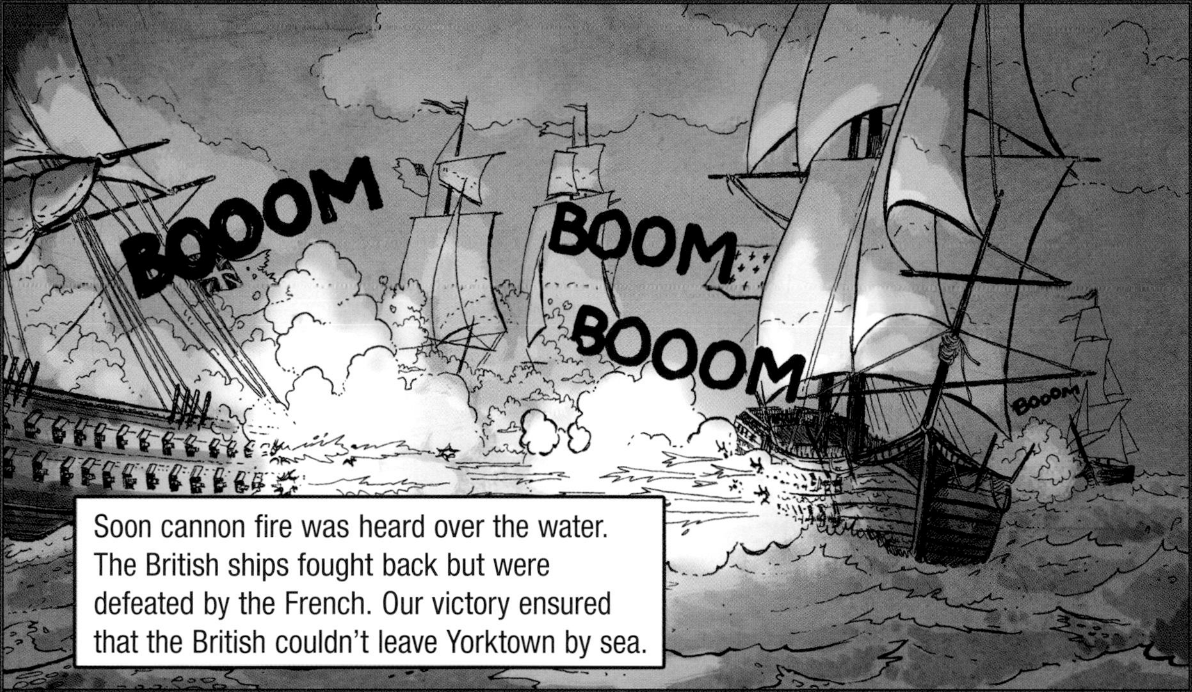
BOOOM
BOOM
BOOOM
Booom
Soon cannon fire was heard over the water. The British ships fought back but were defeated by the French. Our victory ensured that the British couldn't leave Yorktown by sea.

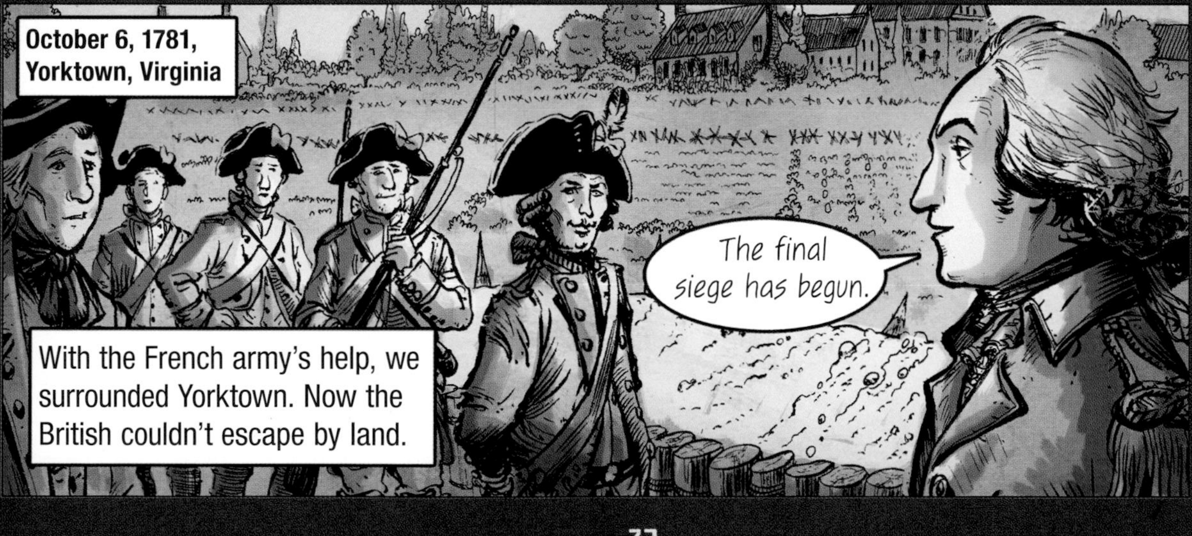
October 6, 1781, Yorktown, Virginia
The final siege has begun.
With the French army's help, we surrounded Yorktown. Now the British couldn't escape by land.

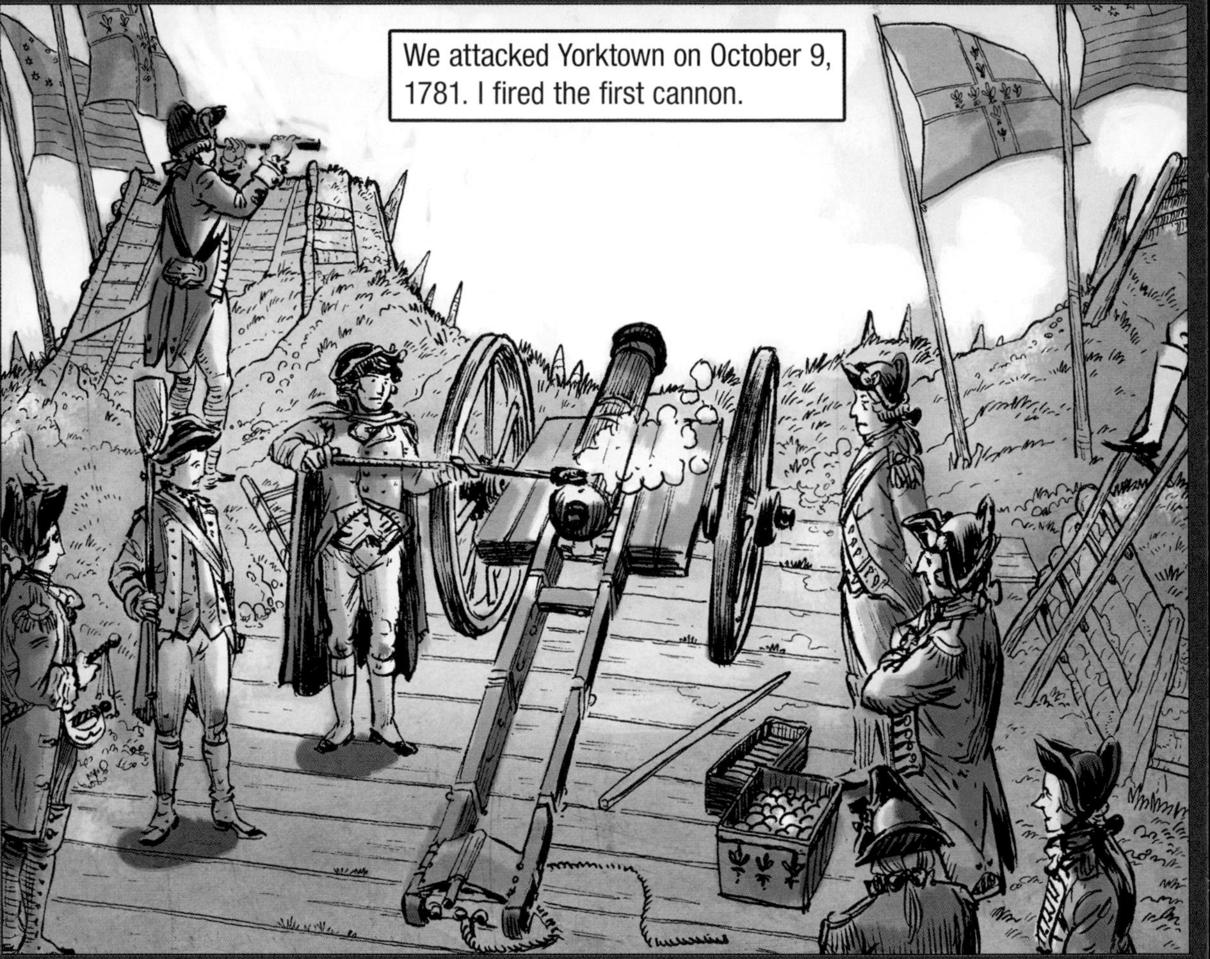
We attacked Yorktown on October 9, 1781. I fired the first cannon.

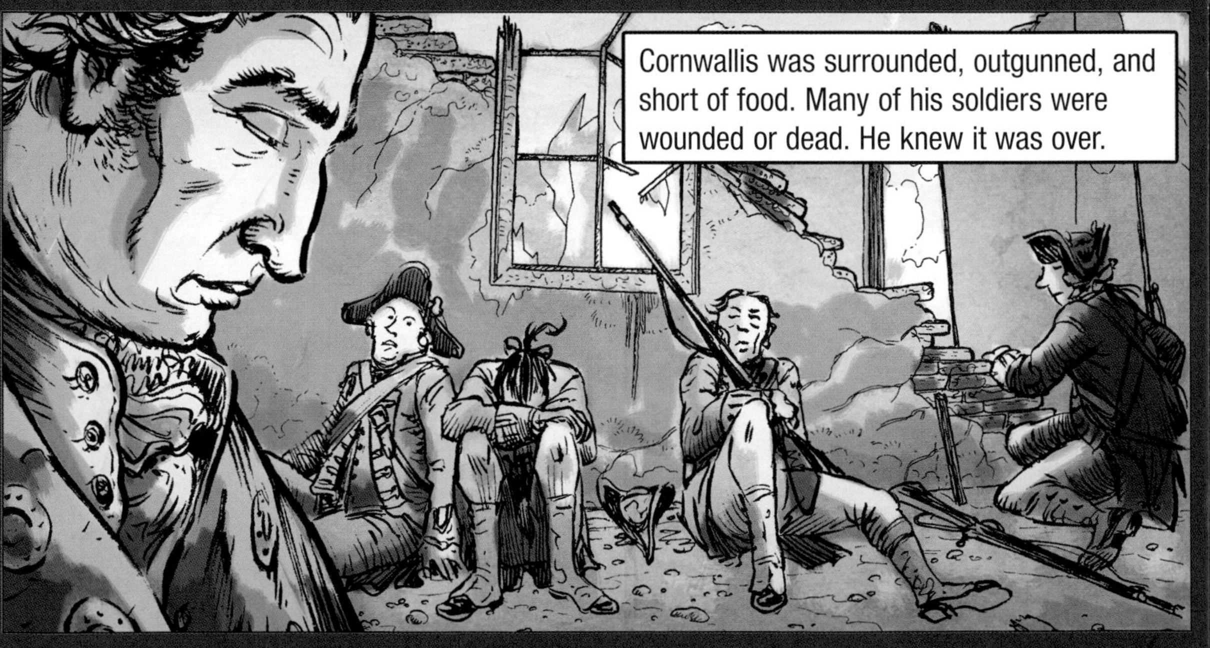
Cornwallis was surrounded, outgunned, and short of food. Many of his soldiers were wounded or dead. He knew it was over.

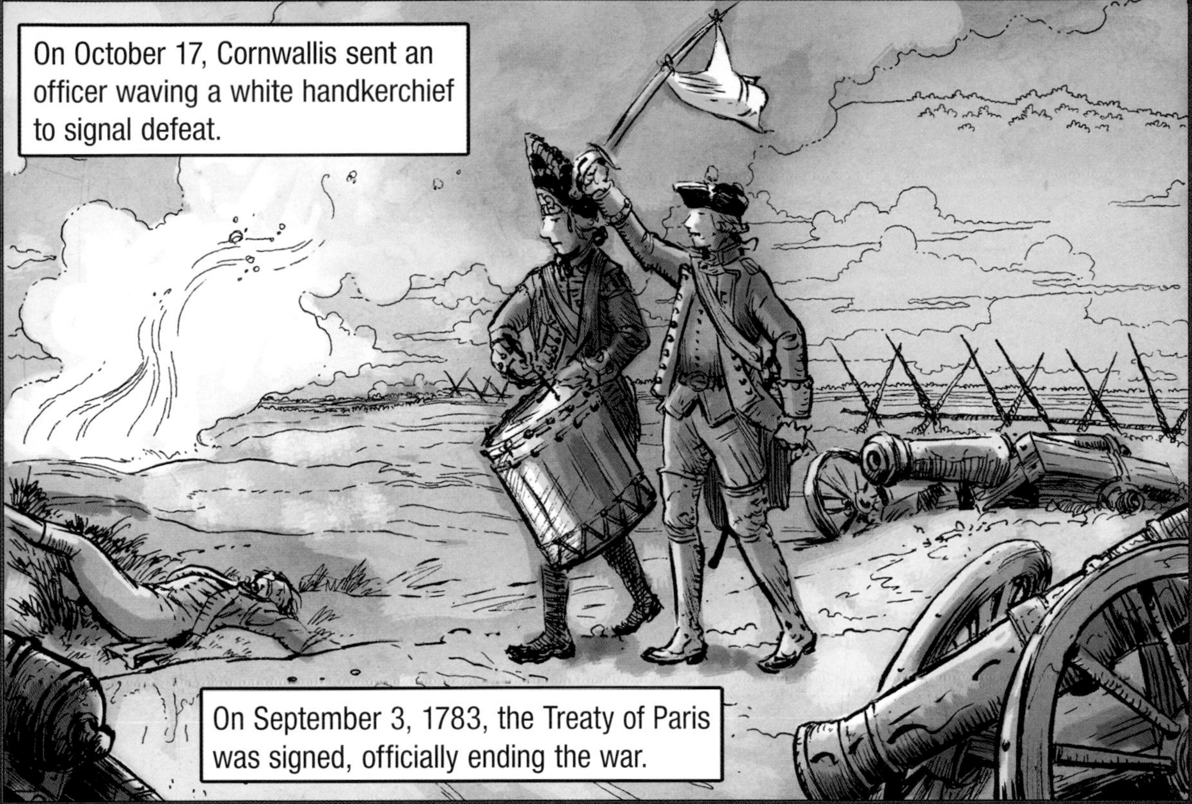
On October 17, Cornwallis sent an officer waving a white handkerchief to signal defeat.
On September 3, 1783, the Treaty of Paris was signed, officially ending the war.

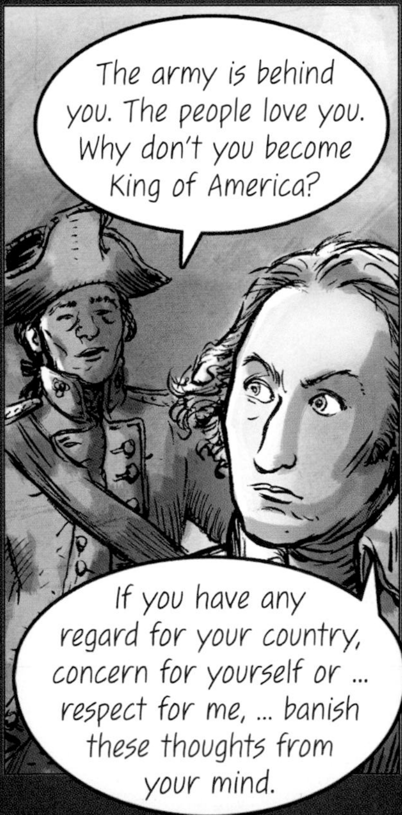
The army is behind you. The people love you. Why don't you become King of America?
If you have any regard for your country, concern for yourself or ... respect for me, ... banish these thoughts from your mind.

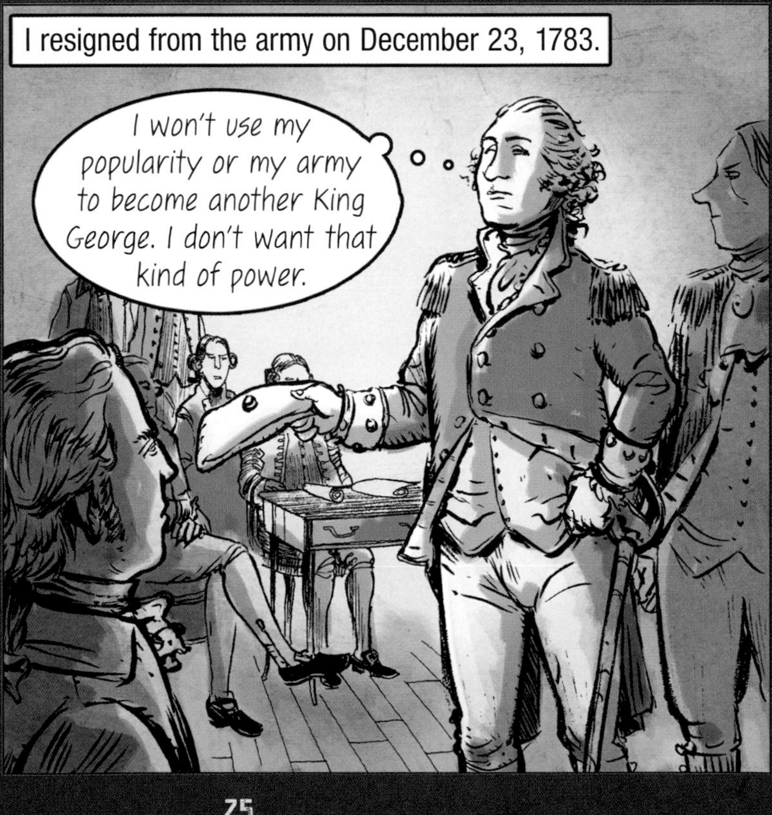
I resigned from the army on December 23, 1783.
I won't use my popularity or my army to become another King George. I don't want that kind of power.

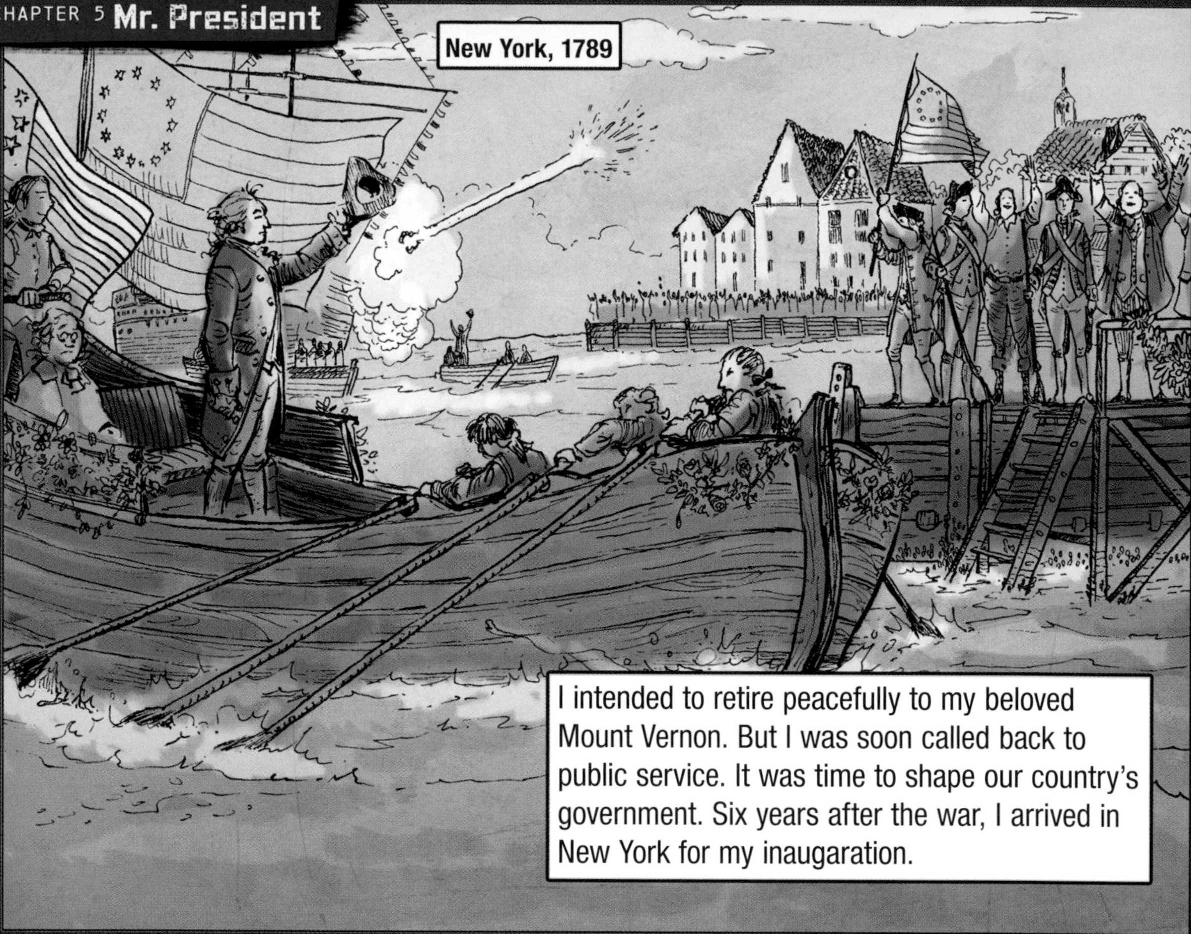
New York, 1789
I intended to retire peacefully to my beloved Mount Vernon. But I was soon called back to public service. It was time to shape our country's government. Six years after the war, I arrived in New York for my inaugaration.

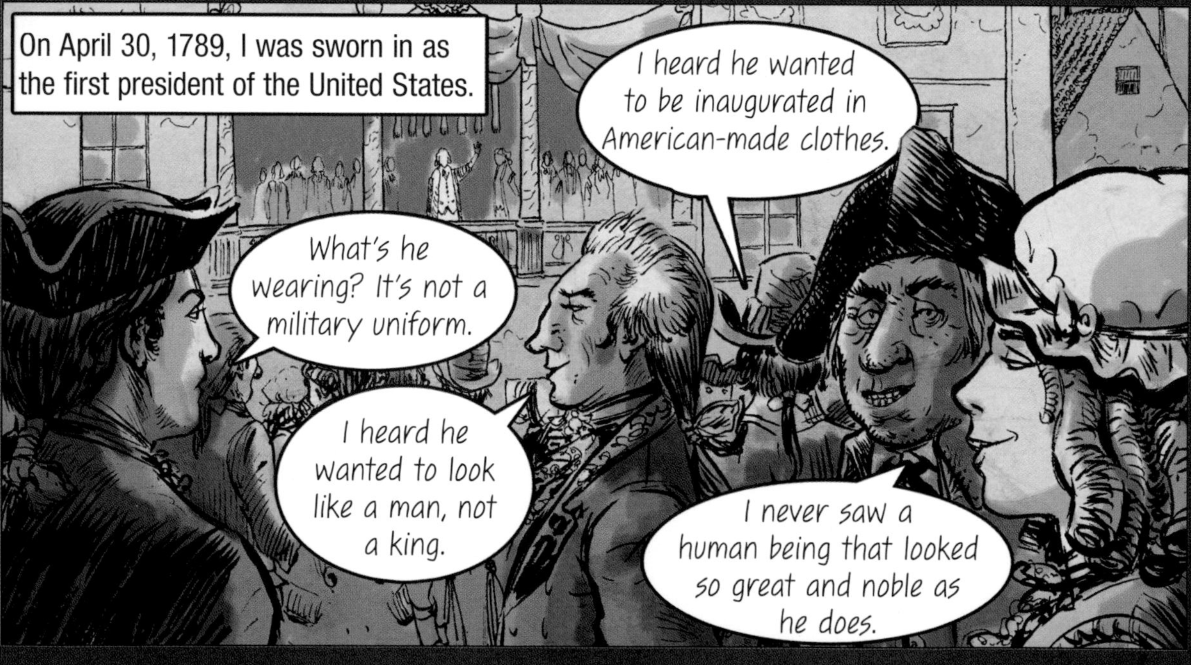
On April 30, 1789, I was sworn in as the first president of the United States.
I heard he wanted to be inaugurated in American-made clothes.
What's he wearing? It's not a military uniform.
I heard he wanted to look like a man, not a king.
I never saw a human being that looked so great and noble as he does.

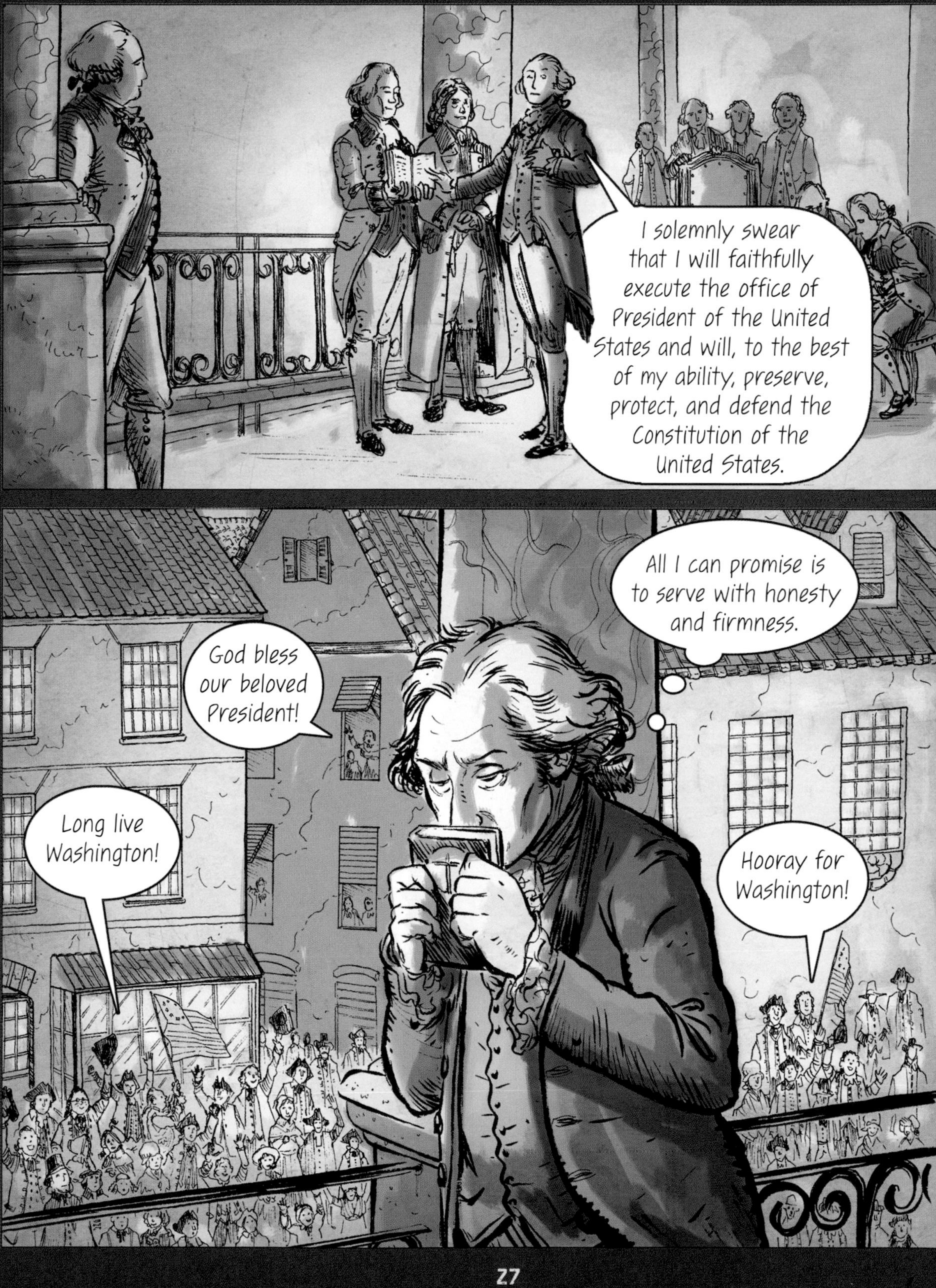
I solemnly swear that I will faithfully execute the office of President of the United States and will, to the best of my ability, preserve, protect, and defend the Constitution of the United States.
All I can promise is to serve with honesty and firmness.
God bless our beloved President!
Long live Washington!
Hooray for Washington!

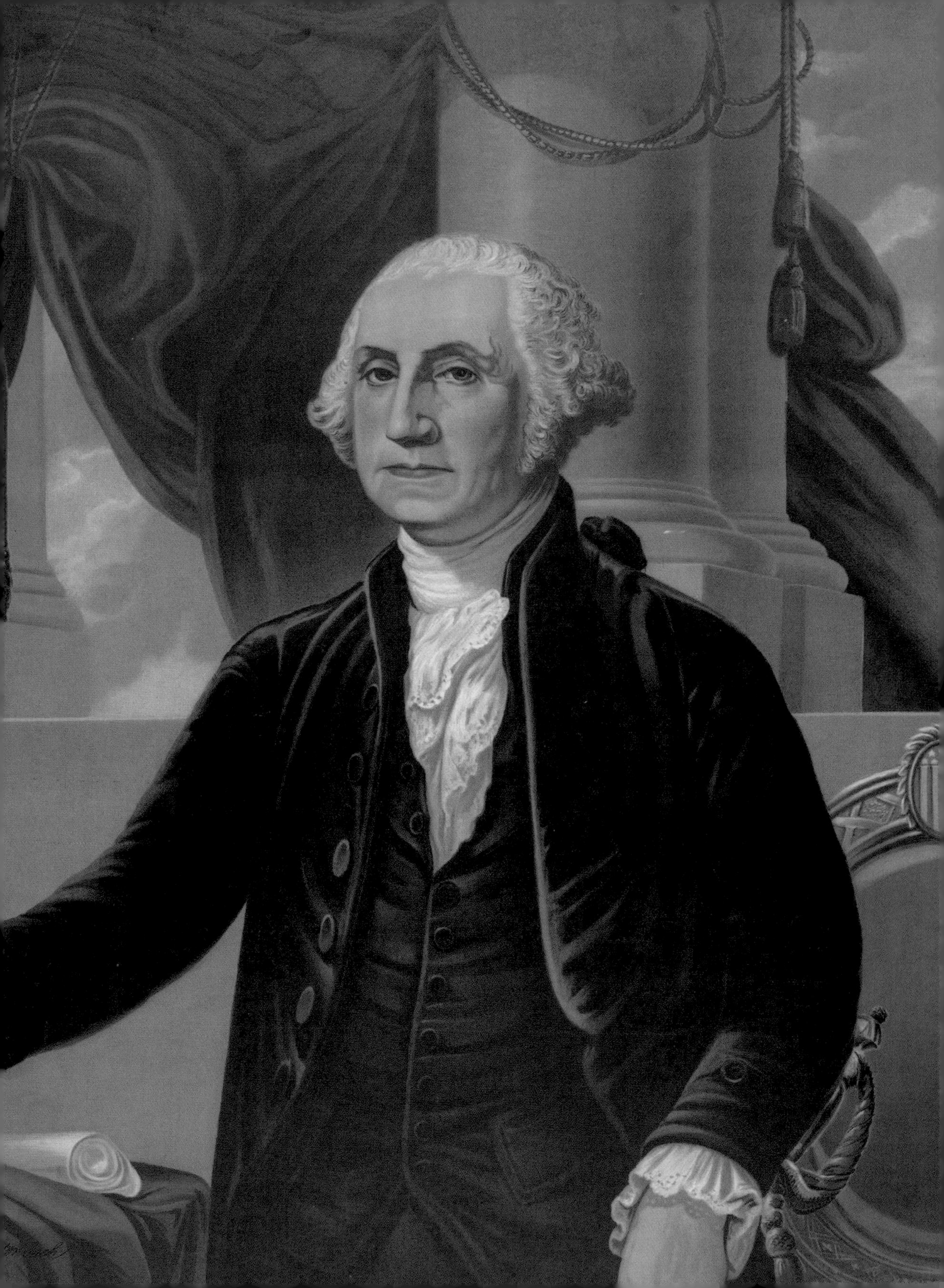

LAST WORDS ON THE
FIRST PRESIDENT

Washington's first term as president began in 1789. He and his advisers had a brand-new government to build. He knew that any move he made would set an example for future presidents.

Washington's first job was to join the states. In the past, the states had acted independently of each other. He knew they needed to work together. He also appointed the first presidential cabinet to help him run the new government. The cabinet included Thomas Jefferson, Alexander Hamilton, and Henry Knox.

In 1791 Washington chose the site of the nation's new capital, which he called the Federal City. It would later be named Washington, D.C., in his honor.

President Washington was unanimously re-elected in 1793. He was so admired that he could have remained president for the rest of his life. But he had seen enough of politics. His actions led to the tradition of limiting presidents to two terms in office, which was held for nearly 150 years.

In 1797 he retired to his beloved Virginia plantation, Mount Vernon. There, he resumed his life as a gentleman farmer.

On December 12, 1799, Washington took his daily ride around Mount Vernon. The day was chilly and wet, and he was out for several hours. He soon became very ill. He died two days later. He was 67 years old. Washington's last words were, "'Tis well."

The entire nation mourned Washington's death. As his friend Congressman Henry Lee stated a few days later, Washington was "First in war, first in peace and first in the hearts of his countrymen." The first president would become known as the "Father of His Country."

GLOSSARY

amputate (AM-pyuh-tayt)—to cut off someone's arm, leg, or other body part, usually because the part is damaged

artillery (ar-TI-luhr-ee)—cannons and other large guns used during battles

colony (KAH-luh-nee)—a place that is settled by people from another country and is controlled by that country

Continental Congress (kahn-tuh-NEN-tuhl KAHNG-gruhs)—leaders from the 13 original American colonies that served as the American government from 1774 to 1789

delegate (DEL-uh-guht)—someone who represents other people at a meeting

deserter (di-ZURT-ur)—a military member who leaves duty without permission

elect (i-LEKT)—to choose someone by voting

import (IM-port)—to bring goods into one country from another

inaugurate (in-AW-gyuh-rate)—to swear an official into public office with a formal ceremony

resign (ri-ZINE)—to give up a job or position voluntarily

siege (SEEJ)—an attack designed to surround a place and cut it off from supplies or help

stalemate (STAYL-mayt)—situation in which neither side of opposing forces can win

unanimous (yoo-NAN-uh-muhss)—agreed on by everyone

READ MORE

Catel, Patrick. *Key People of the Revolutionary War.* Why We Fought: The Revolutionary War. Chicago: Heinemann Library, 2011.

Scarbrough, Mary Hertz. *Heroes of the American Revolution.* The Story of the American Revolution. Mankato, Minn.: Capstone Press, 2012.

Shea, Nicole. *The American Revolution.* Story of America. New York: Gareth Stevens Pub., 2011.

INTERNET SITES

FactHound offers a safe, fun way to find Internet sites related to this book. All of the sites on FactHound have been researched by our staff. Here's all you do:

Visit *www.facthound.com*

Type in this code: 9781429686211

Super-cool stuff! Check out projects, games and lots more at **www.capstonekids.com**

INDEX

AMERICAN GRAPHIC

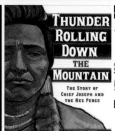